PENGUIN BOOKS

My Psychic Life

Acknowledgements

My darling husband John, you give me strength, you are my best friend at the same time as being my most honest critic. Your love inspires me.

My daughters Rebecca and Fern, you have both been loving and supportive since the beginning, always letting me know you are proud of me: thank you, my darlings.

My dearest friend, manager, agent and business partner Kevin Horkin. You gave my life direction, and your hard work makes everything possible.

A big thank you to Andrew for all his hard work and patience, you were there when I needed you; your advice has been invaluable, thank you.

And last, but certainly not least, Penguin, thank you for this opportunity, your patience and understanding have kept this project fresh and alive for me. I now believe anything is possible if we trust.

My Psychic Life

SALLY MORGAN

PENGUIN BOOKS

PENGUIN BOOKS

Published by the Penguin Group

Penguin Books Ltd, 80 Strand, London WC2R ORL, England

Penguin Group (USA) Inc., 375 Hudson Street, New York, New York 10014, USA

Penguin Group (Canada), 90 Eglinton Avenue East, Suite 700, Toronto, Ontario, Canada M4P 2Y3
(a division of Pearson Penguin Canada Inc.)

Penguin Ireland, 25 St Stephen's Green, Dublin 2, Ireland
(a division of Penguin Books Ltd)

Penguin Group (Australia), 250 Camberwell Road, Camberwell, Victoria 3124, Australia
(a division of Pearson Australia Group Pty Ltd)

Penguin Books India Pvt Ltd, 11 Community Centre, Panchsheel Park, New Delhi – 110 017, India

Penguin Group (NZ), 67 Apollo Drive, Rosedale, North Shore 0632, New Zealand
(a division of Pearson New Zealand Ltd)

Penguin Books (South Africa) (Pty) Ltd, 24 Sturdee Avenue, Rosebank, Johannesburg 2196, South Africa

Penguin Books Ltd, Registered Offices: 80 Strand, London WC2R ORL, England

www.penguin.com

First published 2008

15

Copyright © Sally Morgan, 2008
All rights reserved

The moral right of the author has been asserted

Set in 12.5/14.75 pt Monotype Garamond
Typeset by Rowland Phototypesetting Ltd, Bury St Edmunds, Suffolk
Printed in England by Clays Ltd, St Ives plc

Some names have been changed to protect the identities and privacy of the individuals involved

Except in the United States of America, this book is sold subject
to the condition that it shall not, by way of trade or otherwise, be lent,
re-sold, hired out, or otherwise circulated without the publisher's
prior consent in any form of binding or cover other than that in
which it is published and without a similar condition including this
condition being imposed on the subsequent purchaser

ISBN: 978-0-141-03849-0

www.greenpenguin.co.uk

Penguin Books is committed to a sustainable
future for our business, our readers and our
planet. This book is made from paper certified
by the Forest Stewardship Council.

To all the people in spirit I have been privileged to make contact with, and their relatives that have chosen to see me.

Prologue

Sitting in my office I hear a car pull up, then the *crunch, crunch* of footsteps on the gravel of our drive. You don't need to be psychic to know that the doorbell's about to go . . .

John gets it.

'Hello, love,' I hear him say, 'do you want to come in?'

'Thanks,' she says, and I can hear the nerves in her voice. That's all right. First-time clients are usually nervous. Well, either that or excited; they swing between the two, which is why we never show them straight into the office. Instead, John directs them into the front room, which doubles as my waiting room. They get a chance to gather themselves in there.

Me too. I need a break after an hour of stepping into my last client's life – talking to his dead.

So I go to the kitchen, which is at the other end of the house, where I can stand and clear my head of spirits, shaking away the pain and uncertainty of the reading: souls passed over, shattered relationships, hope and fear.

Just a few moments, that's all I need. Then I pop my head around the door of the front room to greet the client. Let's call her Mary.

'Hello, my dear.'

She's sitting watching the TV. She's slightly startled to

see me there and she gives me the look. Everybody gives me the same look; it's like they want to make sure I'm normal.

'Hello, Sally,' she says. She dithers a bit, as though she's not sure whether to stand up or not.

And then I see the spirit.

Goodness, that's odd – to see a spirit already. Normally it's not until we've taken our seats – when I'm open – that I start seeing them. But sure enough, there at her side is the spirit of a little girl. Such a pretty little thing. She's about seven or eight years old and she has that little-girl-cross expression on her face, as though she's about to stamp her feet. Like she's just been denied sweets.

Except it's not sweets she's angry about. I hear her in my head, this little spirit voice, demanding, 'I want my hair, I want my hair.'

She has all her hair, long and pretty, but even so: 'I want my hair.'

She knows I'm there, she's looking at me. 'I want my hair,' she insists to me, 'it's in a box.'

It's her daughter. Mary's daughter is with her in spirit. My heart goes out to them.

'I want my hair, I want my hair,' says the little girl.

In my head I tell her, 'It's okay, darling, I'll speak to you in a minute. I need to talk to mummy first.'

To her mum I say, 'Do you want to come through, love?'

She follows me through. With her comes her little girl, wearing a pretty pink layered dress.

In the office, Mary sits with her back to the window, the blind half-closed. Outside is my street, rows of houses just like ours, neat front drives and wheelie bins. I'm a psychic in suburbia.

I have a screen in here, like one of those old changing screens – you know the kind of thing I mean. I arrange it across the door as we're chatting, a bit of small talk about where Mary's from. Has she come far? That kind of thing.

For me, it begins with the screen. When the screen goes across the door I'm opening myself to spirit world. Well, usually I am. As I say, it's not normal to see a spirit in the waiting room, but this is one determined little girl. I'm about to find out why.

'Well, it's lovely to see you,' I tell Mary, my back to her as I arrange the screen. I can't see her but I know she'll be using the opportunity to scan the office, which is just like the street, like the house: normal. No crystals, tarot cards or rune stones for me, thanks. If it wasn't for the press cuttings on the wall you'd have no idea what goes on in here.

I take my seat opposite her, watching her visibly relax.

('I want my hair.')

('In a minute, darling, let me talk to mummy.')

'Is this for me?' asks Mary, indicating a cup of water I've place on the table for her.

'Yes,' and by now I'm fiddling with the tapes, unwrapping a tape and putting it in the machine. This is her tape; she can take this away. I click the machine to start recording.

'Now,' I say, 'have you ever seen a medium before?'

'Yes,' she says, and I nod. Most have. But what I know right then is that no other medium has seen her daughter. I just know it.

'You haven't seen me before, though, have you?'

'No. Well, I've seen you on the telly.'

'But you've not seen me one to one, have you?'

She shakes her head no.

'Well, it's very different, darling. Now, do you know what a medium is?'

She's just told me she's been to a medium before, but now says she doesn't know what a medium is. And the funny thing is, they all do this. This whole build-up I'm telling you about, it rarely changes from client to client. Even the extraordinary ones like this one, they all share certain characteristics.

'Okay,' I say, 'so far as I'm concerned, a medium is someone who's in touch with the spirit world. And that's what I do.'

She's nodding.

('I want my hair. It's in a box.')

('Just a second, sweetheart.')

'And you know I also get called a psychic?'

She's nodding. Her eyes go to the press cuttings on the wall: Psychic Sally. Sally the Psychic. Star Psychic. Funny, in newspapers and on the telly that's what they always call me, not a medium; they seem more comfortable with that, as if saying medium conjures up images of people in old houses holding hands around a Ouija board.

To me, it's never really mattered. I'm a medium, but if you want to call me a psychic, be my guest.

'We're all born with psychic ability,' I tell Mary. I can see that she's relaxing now, her whole body posture has changed. 'It's like a natural form of intuition, but certain people can harness it in an everyday way.'

She's nodding.

'And then you get a clairvoyant.'

She smiles and nods.

'Well, the true meaning of clairvoyant is clear view. Literally, it's the ability to see. And me, I've got a bit of all of those things. I'm not saying I'm a jack-of-all-trades, but my work draws on all of those things. Are you all right with that, sweetheart?'

'Yes, yes.' She smiles, takes a sip of her water, pushes her hands through her hair and takes a deep breath.

What usually happens is that as I'm talking, I will be picking up things about the clients. I see their home, their car. I can see the sort of day they've had, or what happened the night before. I can see a row with the boyfriend or with the husband or with the lover. I see everything. It's as though it appears around and behind the sitter. What I get is images, fragments of images, random stray thoughts, snatches of speech. It's like I've switched on the television, turned on the radio, opened a book and started a telephone conversation – all at the same time. It's a bombardment. It's all I can do to control it. I tell them sometimes. I tell them, 'I'd need three mouths to get out all the information I'm getting about you,' and

I see them looking taken aback, wondering if I'm putting them on.

Every now and then, though, you get one that's totally different. One that surprises you. Mary's that one. Because I've already seen her spirit. I knew why she was here from the second I clapped eyes on her.

Bear in mind she doesn't know I've seen her little girl. She doesn't realize I know exactly why she's come.

'You've lost your daughter, haven't you?' I tell her.

The colour slowly drains from her face. When she reaches for her cup of water her hands are shaking and the water slops in the cup. Taking a sip. Putting the cup back to the table. Nodding yes.

Very slowly, as gently and as calmly as I can, I tell her that I can see her daughter. I describe the little girl, seeing her mummy's eyes brim with tears, telling her about the pink layered dress.

'And look, this is very odd,' I say, 'but she's asking for her hair back. She's telling me it's in a box.'

'Yes,' says Mary, 'here, it's in my bag.'

From her handbag she takes out a small green box which she opens on the table. I draw my chair closer to see. Inside the box is a ponytail, tied with a pink ribbon.

She tells me the story. Sophie was an only child and Mary doted on her. She loved to dress her up and comb her hair. But Sophie got cancer and when chemotherapy – tragically unsuccessful – caused her hair to fall out, Mary had kept some of it in a box as a keepsake.

But now here is Sophie, and she's telling mummy, 'I want my hair.'

Now the woman is terrified. I pass her tissue after tissue, consoling her.

'I understand,' I tell her, 'I understand.'

She thinks she's done the wrong thing. She thinks Sophie is angry about the hair.

But no, I tell her. No she's not. Sophie just wanted to see the hair, that was all.

Sophie's quiet. Happy now. Sophie gazes at the hair in the box. I think how lovely it is that she looks so pretty in spirit. She passed over without her hair but the spirit world has returned it to her.

Mary wants to know what she should do with the hair. I tell her I don't know. I can't interpret. I can only tell Mary what I see.

'What do *you* think I should do?' presses Mary.

'I want my hair,' says Sophie.

I pass on the message.

(Some weeks later, Mary told me that she had arranged to have the hair buried with Sophie. After that I never saw Sophie's spirit. Perhaps she was restless and now she's happy. I told Mary that I thought I would have done the same thing.)

When she leaves that day, I take the usual moment or so to compose myself, except it takes longer than a moment. I find myself putting my fingers to my eyes and they come away wet with tears I didn't know I was shedding. Every now and then I have a reading that just gets me – that was one of them.

A few minutes later, three ladies arrive together. More first-time clients. They're the lucky ones – lucky to get an appointment, I mean, because since *Star Psychic* was on TV it's gone mad. We worked out the other day that I've got an 18-year waiting list. That's 72,000 people on a database that my youngest, Fern, keeps. Fern gets through about 100 calls a day, so if you're on the list and you're in when she calls and you can make the slot, then you can see me.

This lot are a bit giggly. One comes in for a reading and I find out later that John caught her friend trying to listen through our downstairs toilet wall. We get that a lot when people come in groups. She tells John she's got an upset tummy. We get a lot of upset tummies in our downstairs toilet.

In breaks between readings I can't take my mind off Mary and Sophie. I think of that little girl in her pink layered dress. I think of the pain Mary feels at losing a daughter.

Because I know it so well, the pain – the pain of losing a child. Mine's not lost to death but to something that sometimes feels even worse – the knowledge that my child is out there making her way in the world, and being unable to reach out to her.

'I understand,' I'd told Mary.

I couldn't do what I do otherwise.

One

'Look at all the flowers, Sal. Have you ever *seen* so many flowers?'

I was four. No, I never had. They lined the hall of the house on Waldemar Avenue. A trail of scent and colour and cards bearing inscriptions that led from the upstairs flat where she had lived, down to the hall, through the front door, then out into the street; out into a Fulham that seemed to stand still, caught in a moment of mourning for one of its best-known faces: my nanny.

Fulham has a hold on me. Always has, always will. Fulham's a part of me; a part of what I do in ways that I'm still trying to work out. Turn off the Fulham Road, go down Waldemar and at number 13 the hold gets stronger still. A stranglehold I sometimes think. I grew up there. I left, but the house beckoned me home and obediently I returned. Every year spent in that house, its hold over me seemed to grow stronger. As though it was constantly beckoning me back to it. In the end it took love to save me from the memories and spirits of Waldemar Avenue.

Someone took my hand. Was it Uncle Tom? No. It was a man, but not Tom; he would have been too distraught. He loved her so much, you see, even though he wasn't actually related to her and wasn't really our uncle

– we just called him that. In fact, he was a lodger at Waldemar, where he'd become friends with her, best friends, really. He was gay, and this in the 1940s and 50s, when you didn't exactly advertise the fact. Terrible, really, what they used to call gay men in those days: poofter, queer; all sorts. Not Nanny, though. She had this way of knowing whether a bloke was gay or not and she wasn't judgemental about it. She danced to the beat of her own drum and as a result they sort of latched on to her, Tom in particular.

So it was not him who was holding my hand. Someone else led me out of the hall and down the three steps to the front yard, to the street outside, where I gazed in awe at the flowers. They were laid on the steps and in the road outside, creating a trail that I followed as I was ushered away. That's what you used to do with kids back then in the early 1950s. When grown-up things like funerals happened you packed the kids off somewhere. We never took part in grown-up business. All I really remember of that day – and it's one of my earliest memories – is sitting on the draining board, the flannel harsh on my face, and the flowers. Everywhere flowers. Because she was so popular, you see, Nanny Gladys. People knew from her newspaper pitch and anyway, that was the way Fulham was back then: everybody knew everybody. Then, it was like a little village. It's different now, of course. There ought to be a sign up: 'Fulham: Not Like it Used To Be', because it's changed. Goodness, so much. I mean, I know all London's changed but Fulham, you think about it, you've got Chelsea on one side, and that's always had its reputation for being a bit hip and trendy. Then there's South Kensington and Knightsbridge and when you think of those two you think posh, you always have.

Fulham, though. Fulham seems to have changed more than either of its neighbours. It's become gentrified. Cosmopolitan. These days housing prices have gone through the roof and you can't move for BMWs and yummy mummies in four-by-fours and posh coffee shops and clothing boutiques. It wasn't always like that. Fulham used to be – well, I suppose you'd say it was working class, which made it a very different place to the upwardly mobile Fulham of today. There were fewer cars, for a start. Not everybody had a car back then. Now, you can hardly get down the streets, with cars parked either side, sometimes double-parked. Take a look at some old pictures, though, and you won't see too many cars – maybe the odd Morris Minor or a bread van. Because of that the streets look wider, the roads not so cramped. They were roads that were safe for kids to play on, and we did, most days. We spent the whole summer outdoors, and not in back gardens, either. (Ours was out of bounds anyway – I'll tell you why in a bit.) No, we were out playing in the street, where the most dangerous vehicles were bicycles carrying grown-ups going to work, or dustmen pushing dustcarts. We had to stay away from Fulham Road, of course. The number 14 bus went along the Fulham Road; there were more cars there, too, and they weren't likely to stop and let you fetch a ball or round off a game of hopscotch. So mainly we stayed round Waldemar.

Which, today, was in mourning.

'All these flowers are for your nanny, Sal,' said my companion, and we stopped for a moment or so on the pavement to admire them. To me, then, they seemed to stretch away for ever. It felt like the pavement was full of them. And if not flowers, then people: men in their black suits, ladies in flat shoes and sober, calf-length coats. Tiny memories of the day: the sound of crying, a match scraping as a cigarette was lit, somebody coughing. On the other side of the street, a man passing removed his hat and bowed his head a little. And then my guardian was taking my hand and leading me away, leaving the house, the funeral preparations, the mourning, behind. The grief, though, at her death; we wouldn't leave that behind for many, many years.

Grandpa George and Nanny Gladys had bought number 13 in 1934, around the time my mother was born: a bay-fronted, three-storey, Edwardian villa in a terrace of other three-storey Edwardian villas. Once upon a time it would have been a single house, but it had been converted into flats and my grandpa bought it with sitting tenants. Mr and Mrs Abel lived in the top flat, and Mrs Spooner was in the middle flat, although she died very shortly before I was born. Others would come and go over the years, our family the only constant fixture.

My mum was born in that house. Her brother, my Uncle Derek, followed four years later. The family were well known in Fulham and Putney because of the newspaper pitches. In those days it was the *Standard*, the *Star* and the *Evening News*. Grandpa George ran four pitches: Putney and the Fulham Road, the bottom of Putney would be taken aback. 'How on earth did you know that, Glad?' 'I dunno, love, I just do.' She'd tell people things about their health they thought nobody knew: 'You want to watch those knees.' She'd know if you were in love and who you were in love with. If you were gay, Nanny Gladys would somehow know. People were in awe of her. She seemed to have this knack of blurting things out.

Just like I would do. If only she'd lived longer, had the life she deserved, she could have helped me. She could have helped explain this ability that would grow within me, getting stronger by the year. She would have known what I was experiencing, sympathized with what I was going through. When I was punished for saying bad things I cried tears of frustration because I didn't mean to be bad, I just said them. I couldn't help it. Nanny Gladys would have understood. Nanny Gladys would have taken my hand and gathered me up and told me not to cry because she had it too – the thing that made you say the bad stuff. Instead, my memories of her are reduced to little fragments, pictures in my mind. I can remember her standing by a fireplace, pulling on a corset and singing; she sang all the time. I remember walking to her, taking early steps. I remember one time, sitting up in bed looking inside a jewellery box and putting something in my mouth, an earring I was later told, and choking on it, my mother trying to clear the airway. The earring lodging in my throat. Coughing and spluttering and choking and crying – even thinking about it now, I find my fingers going to my neck – then my grandmother coming in and lifting me up. She must have got the earring out somehow, and then she was cuddling me. It was her I wanted affection from, I recall, not my mum. But then, she was around me a lot more than my mother was. My mother went to work. My grandmother also worked on the pitches, but early in the morning or at night so she was able to have me in the day time.

Everything else I know about Gladys was told to me by my mum, who mourned her. She mourned her mother so much and probably still does. For years she'd be angry and upset if you even mentioned Nanny. Instead, you had to wait for mum to talk about her. And she would. Eyes gleaming she'd talk about how Nanny used to give tips to the City gents on Putney Bridge; how she used to go into the pub every night and that it used to come alive when she entered. Just one Guinness, she had. She'd sit on her stool at the bar, always the same stool, with her legs crossed and her big high heels on, she'd have her Guinness and then she'd go. Nanny just used to say things to people and the things she said would come true, earning her the affectionate 'Witch of Fulham' name. And like any good witch she even had familiars: two cats, Topsy and Turvy. They were her life; they followed her everywhere. She used to take my mum to work with her, and my mum remembers these two cats waiting on the road for them as they approached. The cats used to purr at Nanny, as though awaiting instructions.

'Come on you two,' she'd tell them, and mum, nanny, Topsy and Turvy would walk along the pavement, the two cats purring happily.

'They're singing to me,' Nanny Gladys told my mother.

They weren't her cats, just cats that she knew, who had taken a shine to her, but that was her all over. She was like a planet around which other, smaller planets circled. I felt it, even then, at that young age – that pull towards her. Whether it was because I somehow, instinctively knew I was like her, the Witch of Fulham, or because that was just her – this huge charisma of hers, I'm not really sure. But I felt that magnetism. Mother used to say that she knew everybody, the tramps at Putney Bridge, even. There was this little park at the bottom of Putney Bridge where the tramps would go, I think it might have been the church giving them food and Nanny would go and give them money. She did it, she said, because she was abandoned herself. Mum said that even if Nan only had a penny in her pocket she'd give it to a tramp or to the Salvation Army.

So, you see, my mother worshipped her. Absolutely worshipped her. When trouble came for my mother, Nan was there for her – and trouble came in 1951, when I was born.

My mother, Beryl, was just 16 when I was conceived; 17 when I was born. She was just a child herself, really. Sorry to sound like a stuck record but 'in those days' you just didn't get pregnant at 16. Well, some girls did, obviously, my mum being one, but you were supposed to get rid of them or get them adopted; there were even places they called 'mother and baby homes'. Pregnant girls were sent away, disowned. Grandpa George went ballistic, apparently. I don't know exactly what he wanted to do with my mum and her baby belly, but I think it was probably along the lines: get it sorted out. There was no doubt talk about bringing shame onto the family, and all that kind of thing. Nanny, though – she was different, wasn't she? As I say, she was ahead of her time. She loved her daughter. There was no way she was going to turn against her. No wonder my mum worshipped her so much. When I was born, there was no mother and baby home for my mum. There were other, different hardships, as I was to discover later in life, but no mother and baby home. My sister Gina followed not long after; there are just 11 months between us.

With Grandpa out working nights on the pitches, the three of us – three generations of the family's women – would often sleep in the same bed, me just a baby, and one night Nanny woke up.

'I'm dying,' she said.

My mother looked at her. She was sitting up at the end of bed, short of breath, repeating the words, 'I'm dying.'

'Oh don't be so stupid,' said my mother, which was what people said back then. After all, Nanny had already been to the doctor twice that week with a sore throat, but the doctor hadn't spotted what was really wrong. He hadn't diagnosed the septicaemia.

'Call an ambulance,' said Nanny Gladys, and maybe there was something in the tone of her voice, or something about the way she looked, but Mother went running to the phone booth on the other side of Fulham Road and called for an ambulance, which took Nanny to the hospital, where she died.

Mum's brother, Uncle Derek, younger than her by

about four years, was working as a delivery boy at the time, and he called round the next morning to find out how Nanny was. My mum answered the door, and screamed at him, 'Mummy's dead.' People in the street stopped and stared: she was crying inconsolably as my Uncle Derek, broken, laid his head against the side of his van and butted the cold metal, moaning, 'No, no, no.' The news quickly spread. Gladys was dead. The Witch of Fulham was dead.

'She can't be dead,' was what they said – so my mum told us over the years. Nobody could believe that Gladys was dead. She was only 41. It's true that people had lower life expectancy in those days, but you didn't drop at 41, you just didn't.

Nan was taken to Mr Brains, the funeral director on Fulham Road. They're still there these days: R Brain & G Gamble and Son.

God only knows what state mum was in for the funeral, I've no memory of seeing her that day. Not her, not Uncle Derek or Grandpa George or even my younger sister, Gina.

What I remember are the flowers.

Later, one of the things mum told me about the funeral was that she saw the two black cats, Topsy and Turvy. They sat on the garden wall, impassive, like two sentinels, and as she watched they each jumped down from the wall. Nobody ever saw them again.

And she mourned, mum did. She grieved for her mother, but so did Uncle Derek, so mum, as his elder sister was cast in the role of his mum. She looked after

Uncle Derek until he joined the Royal Horse Guards and was posted to Cyprus for two years. Every week she made up a parcel for him: sweets, letters, photographs of the family, all lovingly parcelled up and despatched to Uncle Derek. Gina and I were taken to nursery; Grandpa George used to take us on his bike, both of us so tiny we fitted into the basket which held his newspapers. We must have looked such a sight.

Meanwhile, mum got married, to Pat Thatcher, our father. You don't question things at that age, do you? You don't wonder why your mum is marrying your dad. All I remember is the day, little bits of it: memories like camera flashes popping in my head: Flash. Waldemar Avenue. Flash. Everybody's all smiles for a change (because there wasn't much smiling, not in that house). Flash. Somebody telling me that from now on I should call Daddy Pat, 'daddy'. Me forgetting to call him 'daddy', and somebody correcting me, 'No, Sally, it's daddy now,' because it was so important that I called him daddy from now on.

It was 1955. James Dean died that year, his car crashed into another car; Ruth Ellis became the last woman to be hanged in the United Kingdom; Winston Churchill resigned as Prime Minister and Rock 'n' Roll was being born.

And we were a family. My mother, Beryl; father, Pat; sister Gina and me. We lived at Waldemar Avenue, in the basement of number 13, where it always seemed dark, no matter what the time of year.

Looking back now, I wonder if the five-year-old me

had already been dealt the hand I'd play in life. It feels as if all the huge life-shaping events had already taken place, the biggest one being the death of Nanny Gladys and how that affected my mum. It was as though my mum went from being her own mother's little girl to suddenly taking her place, looking after Grandpa, Uncle Derek, her own family; as though Nanny dying robbed her of 10 years of her life. One day, she might want that missing portion of her life back.

Two

Does it all sound a bit grim? Bad spirits and bad memories? Get the violins out for Sally? Sorry if it does. Because it wasn't all grim, you know, it really wasn't. Growing up in Fulham in the 1950s was *fun*. Gina and I were left to our own devices, and it wasn't like it is now, where kids have to be supervised 24 hours a day. These days if kids are out by themselves, chances are they're being neglected and up to no good. Back then, we roamed the streets from noon till night. The world didn't have such sharp edges in those days; you could play out. Imagine that. Playing out.

One of our games was run outs, where you and your friends split yourselves into two gangs, one gang hides, the other has to come looking for you. Back then, you could hide in people's gardens. Either the owners weren't so paranoid about privacy the way they are now or they never caught us, but we used to treat everybody's gardens like they belonged to us, gaining entrance by barrelling through privet hedges. *Ouch*. I remember hiding once, waiting for ages and ages to be found – for what felt like hours, sitting cross-legged, pretty dress around me on the grass (she kept us looking pretty, our mum did, we were like little dolls to her). And I remember sitting waiting to be found and watching caterpillars on the leaves of the privet hedge. Funny, isn't it, that one of my abiding childhood memories is me, my pretty dress and the caterpillars on the privet hedge. I started collecting them after that, we all did it for a while, always hoping to witness that moment when they became a butterfly. Never did, though.

Marbles: we used to collect those as well. We'd play marbles in the gutter. I had a huge collection of marbles. We all did. Another favourite game was hopscotch. We'd chalk up a huge hopscotch board on the road. You used to see them everywhere back then. Now I can't remember the last time I saw a chalk hopscotch board. The other thing we all loved was roller skating. I used to roam my tiny area of London with my roller skates tied together and slung over my shoulder. We were never allowed bikes, of course, not living near the Fulham Road. And tennis balls. I always carried a couple of tennis balls, too, for a game imaginatively called 'Two Balls' that involved, well, throwing two balls, often from hand to hand, although we used to bounce balls off the sides of houses as well, until we got told off by whoever lived inside. There was a gang of us who used to run together, playing run outs and hopscotch and marbles. My best friends were Pamela, Barbara and Margaret, from along the road. There was the Rose family, five of them. Gina was always around, too, only just younger than me, really. Plus any other kids from the area – our bit of the world, Waldemar Avenue, Hestercombe Avenue – just getting up to all sorts: scrumping, that was another thing we used to do. Remember Mr Brains, who ran the funeral parlour? His garden was long and narrow, passing along the rear of the houses on one side of Waldemar, and in his garden were apple trees. We spent so much time in that garden, scrumping apples. I used to collect them and put them in my dress. We'd hide in the garden if we thought someone was coming, crouching in the grass and earth.

'I know you've been scrumping,' said dad, one day.

I stared at him, eyes wide with fear and he regarded me, hard and steely.

'How . . . ?' I said.

'A little bird told me,' he said. He could turn your insides liquid with fear. He spoke so rarely, but when he did . . .

I later realized that he'd seen us from our back garden. He kept pigeons there. Keeping pigeons was his first love, and his coops lined the back wall of our garden, the wall adjoining the Brains' garden. He'd been tending to his pigeons and seen me scrumping. Not that he seemed angry, just careful to make sure I knew he had his eye on me.

We'd come home filthy. I can picture it still. Mum standing on the doorstep, calling us in. She'd be out there ages, shouting for us. During the summer months that's all you'd hear in the evening: mums calling their kids in, getting louder and more hoarse and more frustrated when we failed to appear.

And when we did . . .

'Bloody hell, look at the state of you two. Look at the *state* of you. Where have you been? What have you been up to?'

You name it, we'd been up to it. Scrumping, hide and

seek in the dirt, marbles in the gutter. Staying clean wasn't exactly a high priority for us. Oh, but then . . .

'Go,' she'd point in at the house, into the hallway, her finger saying, Up the stairs. 'Go and get a wash. Get yourselves washed now.'

(I never liked going into the bathroom, I was never comfortable. Like something was in there. And there was, it would turn out later. It was a spirit and it would make me do things. Naughty things I can't tell you about. Because there are some secrets I'll take to my grave: things clients have told me, and what went on in that bathroom. I'm sorry, some things are too personal. Too dark and too frightening.)

'What's this? Have you had a wash?' she'd scream later. She worked during the day; they both did. In those days we were what you'd call latchkey kids. Dad would arrive home first, then mum, and often her first job would be to get us girls clean.

'Course I have.' I'd show her my hands, washed in the sink. 'You bloody little liar. What's all this then?'

There at the wrists was a tidemark. Our arms would be filthy.

Everybody was fanatical about being clean in those days. Well, in our family we were. I remember dad disapproving if we even knocked around with children who weren't as clean as us. 'They're alive,' he'd say of them, the kids who weren't clean. 'Look at them, they're lousy with it, lousy,' and if we turned up after a day out playing, it was, 'Look at their heels.' We wore sandals, our feet would be caked. Dad used to mix up butter and sugar in a bowl, scrubbing our elbows and heels to get the dirt out. Exfoliating them, really.

I remember a woman who owned the delicatessen at the top of the road (unheard of at the time, that was, a *delicatessen*) and she had this big old car with running boards. Do you know the kind of thing I mean? Like a ledge along the door that you could stand on if you wanted. When you watch old gangster films and they make their getaway after a bank job, having shootouts with cops, they're standing on the running boards.

For us, they made a handy hiding place if you were playing a game of run outs, because you could lie along one and not be seen by somebody on the other side of the car. You were off the ground, so if a member of the gang looked underneath the car they wouldn't see your legs. We knew all the tricks. So there I was one day, hiding on this running board, lying flat. There was a shard of broken metal sticking out of the running board. I didn't see it, not until it was too late, and by then I'd gripped it to stop myself from rolling off the running board and it had gone in, piercing me at the base of my thumb on my right hand.

Well, you've never seen blood like it. I was wearing one of my pretty dresses and within seconds it looked like a butcher's apron, soaked in blood.

'Oh my God,' my mum said, when I got home.

I was terrified of her, of course. In those days you were supposed to be terrified of your mum and dad; it was practically the law. So when she screeched, 'What's happened?' I clammed up.

'Nothing,' I stammered. Standing there, with blood all down my front. Blood pouring from the wound in my hand. 'Nothing.'

She bandaged it up. I still have the scar, but she was more worried about the dress than the cut – because that was the other thing back then. Anything less than decapitation was just a minor wound to be treated with a plaster and a clip round the ear. I'll tell you another story about that: on the Fulham Road there used to be this cobbler, Mr Bazman, who was quite famous locally because the jazz singer Cleo Laine had worked in his shop when she was younger, and as a result he appeared in her episode of *This is Your Life* in 1962. Nowadays, you can't walk eight feet in Fulham without bumping into someone from the telly but back then being Cleo Laine's ex-employer was a big deal. Anyway, Mr Bazman's shop was a bit of a kid-magnet around the area. He had this big cellar and we used to play in it; plus, we used to do a trick with the doorbell, which on this particular occasion went horribly wrong for me, because the door closed, *slam*, on my finger.

It didn't hurt. At first it was just numb, but within about 10 minutes it had gone black, the colour of a funeral suit; it throbbed and the pain was almost overpowering as I dashed home, across Waldemar Avenue to number 13.

Once again, I was terrified of what mum would say.

What she said was, 'There's nothing wrong with that. Stop bloody moaning.'

She was wrong, though, it was broken in two places. And you know what? These days I get arthritis in that finger and if I hold my hands up you can see where it was broken; the little finger on my left hand sort of sticks out at an odd angle. No point in bloody moaning, though, that was the thing. You just got on with it. Everybody did.

So that was summer. All the summer months would be spent out in the streets or hiding in people's gardens or getting told off for throwing balls against the sides of houses.

It was different in the winter, though. You didn't go out during the winter months, and mum and dad still worked, so Gina and I stayed indoors, by ourselves. In the morning, mum used to make us some sandwiches, say, 'See you later, then,' and go. During the day dad would often come home at around lunchtime, give us a bowl of soup then go back to work. We used to have friends round and we'd play in the cold hall: hide and seek or schools (I played the teacher) or hospitals, which was always my favourite. Even back then I felt this pull towards the medical profession. From the age of three I'd told mum I wanted to be a midwife. *Three*. Nobody could believe it, she said. Nobody could believe that little three-year-old Sally was talking about being a midwife. Where had I got it from? Three-year-olds don't have any concept of a midwife or what a midwife does, but I, somehow, did. I've got my own theories about that; which I'll come to later.

The next we'd see of mum would be at six, when she got home from work, and it was never as much fun during the winter months. I remember going to bed in the room I shared with Gina in the cold and dark, pulling the covers over me.

I used to dream a lot then. I had a recurring dream – I'd been having it for years – the same dream, where I was in an enclosed space, straining against something that held me in place, and somebody was calling my name. They were calling out, 'Sally,' except in the dream I was thinking, 'Why are they calling me Sally?' Feeling boxed-in, enclosed, struggling against whatever it was that held me there. 'Why are they calling me Sally? My name's not Sally.' I didn't realize it then, but it had started. Whatever it is that allows me to see the things I do had awoken.

Three

I saw my first spirit at nursery. I was four years old.

Grandpa would often pick us up from nursery. We'd ride back to Waldemar perched in his seat. There were times that Mother took us in the pram, but she was working and so was dad. Grandpa was my shepherd in those days.

The nursery was a house, similar to ours, that had been converted by the council. The main nursery was a huge room with a grand bay window, high ceilings, everything big and grand, apart from the tiny children's tables and chairs scattered around, and a rocking horse in the window. It had a really lovely garden with a wooden Wendy house I used to love; I've still got the scar from where one of the boys threw a brick and it hit me, right by that Wendy house.

We used to arrive in the morning and have toast for breakfast. We'd play, and in the afternoons we used to sleep on camp beds laid out in one of the back rooms. On the floor above was where all the tiny babies were looked after, who seemed to spend most of their time in highchairs. If you were ever naughty, the punishment was to sit upstairs with the babies, knowing that downstairs all your friends were having fun in the Wendy house, skipping and colouring in.

I was only ever naughty the once. It was a morning break, and we were all sitting having hot milk in beakers. I can still remember the smell of the plastic beaker. Nearby stood a nursery helper; opposite me a little girl, whose granddad was standing by her side. He wore a hat, a trilby, and a long, black overcoat, and he stood slightly behind the little girl, oblivious of the other children in the room, the noise we all made, eyes only for her. The look on his face was serene. As though nothing in the world pleased him more than seeing his granddaughter drink her milk from a plastic beaker.

'Can I have *my* granddad here?' I said to the helper, who pivoted to look at me, hands on her thighs.

'You what, love?'

'Can I have my granddad here?' I repeated.

'Oh, not yet,' she replied, 'Your granddad's at work. He won't be coming until later, I'm afraid.'

'But she's got her granddad here,' I said and pointed across the table, where the little girl looked at me. Behind her, her granddad seemed not to notice; he just continued looking at her.

'Where?' said the helper, following my finger, frowning.

'Here.' I dropped down off the chair, and hurtled over to her side of the table, reaching out to touch the grand-dad, who at last moved his head, taking his eyes off his grandchild and smiling happily down at me.

Then I was being yanked off my feet, gathered into the nursery helper's arms.

'*There's nobody there*,' she roared, furious. 'You naughty little girl,' my legs kicking as she barked at me, 'Right.

You are going upstairs with the babies. Little girls who tell baby lies go with the other babies.'

'No,' I screamed, still kicking my legs.

I didn't want to go with the babies. I was a little girl, not a baby.

'You're just trying to make us get your granddad,' she snapped, dragging me up the stairs.

No, I wanted to tell her, but was too young to put into words what I felt, which was: what have I done? What have I done that's so wrong I've got to go and sit with the babies?

That's where she put me, though. That's where I spent the afternoon. I still remember it. I remember crying and sobbing and banging my hands and feet. I remember being confused and trying to make sense of what had just happened.

Thinking back now, perhaps that girl's granddad wasn't the first spirit I ever saw. Maybe I'd been seeing them all the time and I remember that one so vividly not because it was the first, but because of the repercussions it had. I'd seen that girl's grandfather. So why did nobody else see him? Why was I being punished?

Four

One night, I woke up with a start, knowing something was wrong, hearing my breathing, quick and frightened in the room, the sound clinging to me, hardly penetrating the dark. And my God it was dark. Deathly black.

I gulped, waiting for my eyes to adjust, looking for the sliver of light that should have shone beneath the door, searching out the curtains and waiting for the normal patterns of light and dark to establish themselves.

That feeling. Something was wrong.

At Waldemar, our family lived on the ground floor and in the basement. There were tenants in the top flats and the first floor flat, but they'd often be empty, people would come and go. On the first floor was the bathroom, so we'd go up there to use that, but otherwise we were restricted to the ground floor and the basement. Imagine taking a traditional living arrangement – kitchen and lounge on the ground floor, bedrooms above – and sinking it by one level. That was us. Our kitchen and dining room were below stairs, underground; off the dining room was a cellar. The whole thing was a cellar really but we called this bit of it the cellar because that was where dad had his workshop and where the coal was kept. Houses had coalholes back then, of course. Ours was outside the front door. Because my granddad on my dad's side was a coalman we were never short of it, and from about August onwards he'd make sure the cellar was always stocked. We needed it. The way you got warm back then was with a coal fire. Everybody had them. But the smog they created. Let me tell you about that smog.

I remember walking to school – Munster Road Primary School – aged about seven, eight and nine, and the smog was so thick, so noxious, that you had to tie a scarf around your face and secure it at the back. It was wrapped twice around your face. The smog was so bad in the mornings you couldn't see your hand in front of your face; couldn't see your way to school. Gina and I would be with Pamela and Barbara, who were older than we were, and it was their job to lead us to school, the four of us in a convoy, scarves wound tightly around our faces. Slowly, carefully, smog billowing around us, we'd feel our way to school, using the garden walls to guide us.

It was like that right up until the Clean Air Act in 1968, when everybody had to use smokeless fuels, and factories were forced to build taller chimneys. We all had fires, you see, which is why the smog got so bad. Everybody had fires going from first thing in the morning till last thing at night, and our house was no different.

Except not this particular night.

The house was cold. The fire had gone out. Then, Gina and I shared the bedroom with my mum and dad. They slept in the big bed; Gina and I topped and tailed in a smaller bed. What I knew, lying there in the dark, hearing the silence settle around me, was that mum and dad were not in the room with us. There was no chink of light from beneath the door. No sound of a radio or television from downstairs. No sound of my parents talking, eating, or doing the dishes. None of the usual night-time clatter.

There was just that awful, clinging silence.

I got out of bed, saying, 'Hello?' very quietly into the room.

Nothing in reply. Gentle snoring came from my sister at the other end of the bed. Outside in the road, I think I heard the sound of a single car slowly putt-putting down Waldemar, making the turn into Hestercombe. I padded to the bedroom door, twisted the handle and opened it, peering out into the hall.

It was pitch black. The hall was silent. All signs of life were dormant. I felt a little whimper in my throat, the beginnings of tears, and bit them back.

'Hello?' I said, more to hear myself than in the hope of a reply.

The lino was cold on my toes; the sticky sound of it on my feet accompanied me as I stepped out of the bedroom and into the hall, reaching out a hand to feel my way along, just as we would on the smog-filled journeys to school. Only now I had nobody to guide me; no older girls to make sure I was safe. All I had was the touch of my hand on the wallpaper. The feel of it – I remember it so clearly, the embossed paper, leaves or flowers that bloomed reassuringly beneath my fingers as I felt my way along the hall, hearing only my own feet on the lino and my breathing. In daylight the wallpaper was a brown colour. Tonight it was black. Everything was.

Behind me was the staircase, a huge, ornate flight of

stairs leading up to the first floor and the flat there. I glanced back but saw nothing, just the foot of the stairs, listening for activity from the flats above. Up there, it was musty. Up there was the flat where Mr and Mrs Abel lived. Mrs Abel used to wear this huge fox-fur thing, a sable that she draped around her neck. I remember being fascinated by it; fascinated by its legs in particular. And what a character Mrs Abel was. She'd always go out with a big hat on, and wore huge dresses. I used to ask my mum why she had such long dresses on, because they would go down to the ground; she was like something out of a bygone era, dressed like Queen Mary, carrying an umbrella with her everywhere she went – an umbrella with a handle in the shape of a duck's head. There were so many fascinating things about her. Me, a young child, I was transfixed by her and I think she knew it.

'Come up and see Mr Abel,' she'd say, beckoning me to climb the stairs, past the first floor, up another flight of stairs, and into their flat, the place like a darkened drawing room out of a novel. At the windows were thick, red curtains hanging from a huge, brass curtain rail, a round table over which hung a crushed velvet tablecloth, a fire roaring in the hearth and Mr Abel, sitting, holding a pipe to his lips, the pipe stalk disappearing into his silver moustache. The room smelt of his pipe and, as Mrs Abel bent to talk, the parma violets she always used to eat. Once, Gina and I had chicken pox or measles – I can't remember which. Mum had gone to work so we were in the bedroom, suffering with our spotty disease. We had colouring books spread out on the bed and there was a television in the room, perhaps moved in there especially for us, and we were sitting watching *The Woodentops*. We both loved that; we were sitting rapt, when the handle went and Mrs Abel from upstairs popped her head around the door.

'I've bought you a new sweet,' she told us, beaming, and we bounced, happy, as she produced two bars of Milky Way, the *brand new* chocolate bar.

'Ooh,' she said, 'look at you, you're covered in spots. Are you itching? Don't you go scratching them, will you?' Fussing over us a little, and because we were two poorly little girls, left with just colouring-in and the TV, we basked in her concern. She brought us Lucozade, too. Mum had asked her to, I think, because in those days Lucozade had a reputation as a cure-all wonder-drink. Gold, fizzy medicine. It came wrapped in crinkly gold paper and you put a bottle of it by your bed when you were ill.

It can't have been long after that illness that Mr Abel died and Mrs Abel moved out. That crinkly stuff on the bottle of Lucozade always reminds me of her.

Apart from her visits, we'd be alone all day in that bedroom when we were ill. Mum would leave us a bucket in case we needed to go to the toilet because we weren't to go downstairs to the outside loo when it was so cold. To get there you'd have to cross the hall, open the door to downstairs, go out through the kitchen and scullery, out across the concrete . . .

I opened the door now.

I was used to feeling the warmth of the fire from down

below, hearing canned laughter from the TV. Nothing. Silence.

'Mummy?' I called down the stairs. The chill I felt wasn't just the cold. 'Mummy.'

There was no reply. The house closed in on me and once again I felt the beginnings of tears, wanting to cry, feeling panic tickle at my insides. I was thinking, 'They've gone. Mummy and daddy have gone,' and desperately trying to ignore a fearful voice inside telling me, *They've left you. They've left you and you'll never seem them again.*

Worse: *mummy and daddy are dead.*

In the dark hall I heard myself whimper.

I could build a fire. I could do that. What I'd do, I'd line the hearth with balled-up pages from the *Standard*. I would get the fire roaring by throwing sugar on it.

But I couldn't see. Too small to reach the light switch. If the meter had run out I had no sixpence for it. Now I let out a sob, the sound reaching Gina, who woke and started crying. The way my mother had become the surrogate mum for Uncle Derek when Nanny Gladys died. That was how I was with Gina when mum was working or, like now, just not there.

I wanted to find light. I was thinking, 'I have to open the front door. I know I'm going to get told off, but I have to open the front door because there'll be light if I open the front door. Light from the lamp in the street.'

'Come on,' I told Gina, and the two of us walked, bare feet on the cold lino, to the front door, which we opened, grateful for the street lamp, and sat down on the step to wait for mummy and daddy.

We were five or six. We sat on the doorstep, the two of us crying, for what felt like hours, until Mr Whitfield appeared from inside the fog. He lived down the street. He worked on the railways and he'd come home late. He must have done shift work, thinking about it.

He appeared out of the fog and said, 'Hello, you two.'

He was a strong man, and he picked us both up and took us into the hallway. He smelled of metal and oil and coal fires. He held us to him as he walked into the hall and called for mum and dad, then Sheila, who lived in the flat above.

'Oh, don't worry, it won't happen again,' she was telling him as we were taken upstairs, exhausted from crying on the doorstep. 'I'll tell Beryl, they'll be home shortly.' The next thing I remember is being carried down the stairs in my dad's arms, and him putting me in bed, telling me, 'You must never do that. You're going to get us into trouble, you mustn't do that.' Exasperated, probably, as they'd arranged for Sheila to listen out for us. People did that in those days and Sheila was only on the floor above, after all. But of course we didn't know about that arrangement. We had just woken up feeling alone and frightened. Now we were worried that we'd got our parents into trouble, because when you're young, you think everything is your fault. If you slash your hand on a car running board you think you'll be in trouble for being there in the first place; my broken finger was my fault because we shouldn't have been playing tricks on Cleo Laine's friend Mr Bazman the cobbler; and it was our fault we were seen by Mr Whitfield and taken upstairs to Sheila's flat.

As a child, you have all this guilt thrust upon you. Undeserved. It takes years to deal with it.

These days in my work I see that so much. I have clients wracked with remorse for things they think they've done to people now in spirit. You know what I find myself telling my clients more than anything else? Words to the effect that: 'He says you shouldn't feel guilt. That you shouldn't worry. That you did all you could. That you were there for him.' I help them deal with their guilt. To do that, I've had to deal with my own. Because it happened again. And we did get up. I knew we shouldn't go to the front doorstep again, sit there crying like two little waifs. I'd been told it would get them into trouble. But I couldn't help it. And Mr Whitfield came home from work and saw us crying on the step and said, 'Oh no, not you two *again*.'

Saturday nights, it happened. My mum and dad were so young, you see. They were barely out of their teens. It was the 1950s. Also, it was a different era. In those days you could leave kids more than you can these days. What I'm saying is: I don't blame them and I'm not trying to say they were this, or that, one thing or the other.

They were just a young couple, coping with being young parents, holding down jobs – in my mum's case dealing with the grief of losing her mother. And as I keep saying, things were different back then.

Five

It wasn't long after that night that the lights started coming on.

It was in the winter that it started. If it was cold or raining hard, we weren't allowed to use the outside loo, which was just a quick dash from the back door. Instead, we had to venture upstairs, and I remember the first time it happened, the thing with the lights. It was on one of those dark, cold London nights, rain sheeting down, slapping against the scullery window.

'I need the loo,' I said.

'Not out there,' said dad, flatly. We were all watching TV. Mum and dad sat at the kitchen table, Gina and I on the little rattan stools we had. As usual, a fire roared in the grate.

'Where then?'

'You'll have to go upstairs,' he said, eyes never leaving *Steptoe and Son*. 'Go upstairs, use the bathroom up there.'

Just what I was worried about. I'd have preferred to brave the cold and wet rather than that. It was a right mission. It meant I'd have to run up the stairs to the ground floor, then into the long, cold and draughty hall with its lino-covered floor and embossed brown-painted wallpaper, and from there I had to go up the creaky stairs to the bathroom. Mum and dad were both fanatical about switching the lights on and off, the same as everybody in those days, so when I got to the hall I had to switch on the hall light (standing on a box and still I could only just reach), then dash to the loo and do my business (ignoring the feeling I always got in the bathroom; the way my head went fuzzy when I was in there), then back downstairs to the hall, pause, switch off the hall light on the way back down and then settle back into my rattan stool. Phew.

Dad would look at me, saying nothing. He'd have listened for the sound of the light switch, satisfying himself I hadn't left a light on.

So, with the laughter from *Steptoe and Son* behind me, I ran up the basement steps, stepped through the door at the top and into the dark hall. For a moment or so I stood by the door, letting my eyes adjust, hearing the reassuring sound of the television from down below, trying not to let the dark panic me. Then I darted towards the stairs, about to climb up on the box, stand on tiptoe and flick the . . .

The lights went on. I stopped in my tracks and heard myself say, 'Oh,' as the hall was transformed, suddenly bright and almost welcoming. I looked at the light switch. The huge, brass light switch. It was still in the off position. I hadn't touched it, yet the light was on.

Shrugging, I ran up to the toilet, did my business then dashed back down again, pausing at the light switch, thinking, 'What do I do now?' Because if I flicked the light switch that would be flicking it to the on position, and the light was already on.

I was doing all but scratching my head, trying to work

out this puzzle, when the lights made my decision for me and turned themselves off.

Ah. In my mind, I thanked them. Looking back now (because, weirdly enough, it's not something I thought about much at the time), it's like the house helped me. It lit my journey.

I trotted back down the stairs and took my seat in my rattan stool. My father turned his head to look at me.

'You put the lights on?' he asked.

'Yeah, course,' I replied.

His eyes narrowed. He hadn't heard the lights go on.

'And you turned them off again?'

'Yeah.'

His eyes narrowed further. He knew I couldn't make it to the toilet without a light but he hadn't heard the tell-tale click of the switch.

Slowly he rose from his seat, walked to the door, then went *thump, thump, thump,* up the stairs to check the light was out. Returning, he gave me an odd look as he took his seat, back to watching *Steptoe and Son* and instantly roaring with laughter at 'You dirty old man,' Harold's catchphrase. But that look he gave me as he sat down was a mixture of puzzlement, curiosity and suspicion. I didn't know it then, but I would have to get used to that look as I grew older.

It happened again. Matter of fact, it happened almost every time I went to the toilet. I'd get up to the hallway, the lights would come on, wait until I'd done what I needed to do, then flick off again. Sometimes they'd wait, as though to taunt my dad. I swear on two or three occasions, they'd stay on, while downstairs our little pantomime would begin.

'Lights.'

'They're off.'

'They'd better be.'

He'd rise from his seat and climb the steps. I'd be gulping, wondering if the lights had switched off. He'd open the door . . .

And that very second, *poof*, the lights would go out.

Returning, he'd say to mum, 'We've got to get the electrics fixed in here.' From her seat mum glanced over at me, seeing what, I don't know – Nanny Gladys, perhaps. From dad I got that same look: puzzlement, curiosity, suspicion.

Don't think for a second that I was getting one over on my dad, though. Or that I was trying to wind him up. I was young but I wasn't stupid. Sure, mum would give us a clip round the ear, but it was dad we were really frightened of. He was very quiet, but when he lost his temper he'd shout, and to us, then, it sounded like all hell had broken loose. I mean, they were different times, and attitudes to punishment and discipline have changed so much since then but like most kids, my sister and I grew up knowing we'd get a clout if we were naughty. And it would hurt, too.

He was a plumber, and worked for the same firm all his life. He went everywhere by bike; to this day he has never learnt to drive. A giant of a man, fearsome and terrifying, he had a reputation in Fulham when he was younger, as he used to knock about in a gang. He'd be one of those hanging around outside the town hall where the dances were held in the late 1940s and early 1950s. Everybody used to want to fight him, mum said, because he was a big fella, and he could handle himself, but wouldn't say two words. You know what blokes are like. They saw that as a challenge, and wanted to have a pop at my dad. But he never lost. One time, he was in a brawl in Fulham Broadway and hit this bloke who ended up unconscious on the deck of a bus. Only he stayed unconscious so when the bobbies arrested my dad they tried to get him to admit that he'd hit the man with a piece of wood or something, but when the guy came round he told the police that my dad had hit him with his fist. Fair's fair.

You didn't want to mess with my dad. Even now he's retired and settled down. I bet he could still handle himself.

Yet he loved animals. Every night he had a ritual. He'd come home from work and the first thing he did was see to his birds. This was out in the back garden. Gina and I weren't allowed to go there, but dad's pigeon coops lined the garden boundaries; you'd hear them there when you went to use the outside loo, but that was as close as you ever got to them – we weren't allowed any further than the outside loo. So, first he'd see to the pigeons, doing whatever he was doing – it was all a complete mystery to us – feeding them, talking to them. I know one thing: my dad spoke to those bloody pigeons far more than he ever talked to either Gina or me. Next job on his list would be hosing down the back yard, which the dogs used for their toilet. And oh, the dogs. We had so many of them over the years, whippets mainly. Mum and dad bred them as a sort of second income. We had a boxer, too, Brandy, and the only time I've ever seen my dad cry was when Brandy died. She got cancer in her kidney and had to be put to sleep. At the time it was dreadful. My dad was devastated, but we all were, we all loved Brandy; on cold mornings she used to take hold of my nightie and drag me into her basket, to keep me warm. What a dog she was. Then there were Flash, Sheba and Pandora, and the hundreds of pups they produced.

After he'd done the animals he'd sit down to watch a bit of telly. Then, the signal: 'I'm going to have a wash.' Which meant we'd have to stay out of the kitchen for an hour while he had a strip-wash and shave. I can still remember his container: flannel, bar of Lifebuoy soap inside. He'd remove his vest to wash and when he was finished he'd put on a new vest then settle down in front of the telly to eat his meal. By that time mum would have arrived home. She got home about six pm, a couple of hours after him, and she'd make the meal, walk the dogs, and dad would sit and watch telly or go off into the cellar, which acted as his workshop, where he'd make ornate bird cages.

Saturdays were special. On Saturdays he'd race the pigeons, or take them to the shows. Often in the evenings, he and mum would hold a party, at mum's insistence, not surprisingly; she absolutely loved a party, and was as gregarious and sociable as he was withdrawn and tight-lipped. But he joined in, bless him, and together they'd clear out the basement, pushing what little furniture we had to the sides, and she'd invite her friends from work.

She was so young when she had me, of course, and she never really wanted to let go of her youth. That was why she loved her parties so much. Her holidays, too. Dad would never have a day off work, so it was mum that took us on holidays, camping in Devon and Cornwall. He couldn't complain because she was the main bread-winner. They both worked hard, but mum had the higher-ranking job; secretarial positions, in admin, she used to run whole departments. Dad was a simple bloke, happy with cycling to work, coming home, looking after his pigeons and taking a bath once a week: it was the way it was done back then. Not affectionate or demonstrative. He never had a word for anyone. Mum, she was the fiery one, very intelligent, ambitious and outspoken. As quick with a kiss and a hug as she would be to flick the back of your legs with a dog lead when you'd been naughty.

And she was powerful. She was able to influence those around her because she'd inherited my Nanny's charisma. I always felt there was something of Nanny's witchiness in her: people would find themselves under her spell, and nobody more than me. Being the eldest of her two daughters, it would be me she spoke to, and not like a little girl, either, but more like a friend. I'd hear stories about Nanny Gladys and dad; stories about her own past. She'd often tell me much more than I ever wanted to hear – like graphic details of how I was conceived. She told me more than she probably wanted to, and little by little, over a period of years, of *decades*, really, the truth would begin to emerge . . .

I haven't spoken to my mum for 12 years. The seeds of that situation were being sown way back then, in the early 1950s in the dark basement at Waldemar Avenue.

Six

One particular day I was sitting on the outside loo, singing, 'La, la, la,' when I saw a woman standing in front of me. I looked at her for a moment or so, my mind racing. Had I closed my eyes? Did the door go and I didn't hear it? Why was there a woman standing there?

No, she wasn't standing, she was hovering. A single thought came to me: Those aren't mummy's feet. I looked from her feet to the rest of her. She was an old lady, face creased with age, grey hair in a bun. She held her hands outstretched, like an opera singer, her sleeves pulled up. She wore a large white apron tied at the middle, dropping to within an inch or so of her skirt hem, ankles, then shoes – and then nothing. Empty space. She actually hovered in the air in front of me.

My mouth dropped open, the song stuck in my throat as she leaned forward slightly, as though to tell me something very important.

And she did. She said, 'Pull your knickers up and get in. It's cold.'

'What's the matter?' recoiled mum as I came racing through the kitchen door seconds later. It was the fastest I'd ever made that trip, I can tell you.

Breathless, shocked (but not scared exactly; I was never scared by the things I saw growing up, only in the bath-

42

room) I blurted, 'There's a woman in the garden, she's dressed funny and she told me to pull my knickers up and get in.'

Slam. Mum was out of the door, reappearing a moment later, telling me what I already expected to hear: that there was nobody out there.

'What did she look like?' she asked, coming down to my level and clasping my shoulders. I told her. I told her about the bun and sleeves pulled up and about the apron. She straightened, some colour leaving her face.

'That was my grandmother,' she said.

Her grandmother. My great grandmother. Nanny Brodie. My mother began to cry. I'd described her perfectly, she said. That had been Nanny Brodie standing in front of me, she was sure of it.

'Pull your knickers up,' Granny Brodie had told me. I'd been daydreaming on the loo, you see, sitting out there in the cold. The way I like to see it now is that Granny Brodie caught sight of me from spirit world; saw me sitting out there, perhaps about to catch a chill, and appeared to me to chivvy me along. It certainly worked, plus she wasn't needed again; I didn't dawdle after that. It works that way with spirits sometimes. They appear for as long as they're needed and no more. Like the lights. They did their automatic switching trick for a couple of years and only stopped when I was tall enough to reach the brass light switch. Who knows, maybe that was Granny Brodie's doing, too. There was a time when I was younger, and I was walking beneath an ironing board. Yet again, this is one of my earliest memories, but I remember it well because I put my hand up to grasp the side of the ironing board and felt a slap, just as if my mother had been standing there, gasping to see my little hand so near the iron and slapping it away.

Except it wasn't my mother who'd slapped my hand. She was in the kitchen making dinner. There was nobody else in the room. Not on this plane anyway.

Though Granny Brodie may have been with me in spirit that day, she didn't belong to the house. There were others who did, though; the one I saw on the stairs, for example.

It happened on a day when we were playing in the hall, which we often did. I can't remember what we were doing but I recall being compelled to turn around, sensing something behind me – something on the stairs. There was a woman on the steps.

I stood in the middle of the huge hall, a little girl in a pretty dress. I must have been seven at the time. She wasn't standing, like Granny Brodie had been. This woman was sprawled on the stairs, head facing down towards the hallway, her arms and legs splayed out. She wore a long grey skirt, thick grey tights and lace-up black shoes. She was almost transparent; I could see the stairs beneath her. Her eyes were still, empty and lifeless.

I stood and looked at her for a moment or so, then turned around to continue playing with my sister, saying nothing. Mostly, I didn't tell people what I'd seen; I'd learnt not to – I found I got in trouble, got called a liar or a naughty little girl – but much later that night, I told my mother, and once again I saw her eyes widen, colour draining from her face.

'What did you just say?' she snapped.

'That I saw this woman the wrong way on the stairs. And her arms and legs were all sticking out like this . . .' I stood in our dining room, making grotesque shapes with my arms for my mother's benefit.

'Bloody hell,' she said, 'you know who that was, don't you?'

'Who?'

'Mrs Spooner. That was Mrs Spooner you've just seen – who used to live in the middle flat.'

Mrs Spooner had been one of the sitting tenants when Grandpa bought the house. She was there at Waldemar for years but died just days before I was born. One day when mum was heavily pregnant with me, she was in one of the bedrooms when she heard a scream from the hallway and came running out to see Mrs Spooner on the stairs. Mrs Spooner had tripped and fallen, breaking her neck. Her arms and legs were splayed out. She was wearing a long, grey skirt, grey stockings and black lace-up shoes.

Mum had thought she was going to go into labour, there and then, with the shock of seeing Mrs Spooner on the stairs. Years later I'd seen the same thing, turned and gone back to playing with my sister.

'You were in my womb,' said mum. 'Oh my goodness,' she gasped, as though she'd suddenly solved the puzzle; like she suddenly understood how her Sally saw the things she saw. 'You were in my womb. That must be how you saw it.'

I said nothing. I could see what she wanted to believe.

Some instinct made me realize that it was best for me if she carried on thinking that way. But I knew what I'd seen. I'd worked out now that these weren't real people. They were spirits. Like the little girl's granddad at nursery. Like Granny Brodie. Ghosts only I could see.

Seven

I used to get very ill when I was little. Back then I had a shadow on the lung so I suffered from a terrible whooping cough. Like an annual event – winter must be here because Sally's got the whooping cough. And it was awful every year. A nurse used to have to come each morning to give me injections. Then, one particular winter, it became even more serious. I became really ill and my parents started to worry that it was polio, which was going round at the time, claiming the lives of children my age.

We knew when we were really sick because mum and dad moved us to their room, sometimes even into their bed. I lay there aware of an atmosphere in the house: dread; a constant worry in the air as they monitored my condition. I remember seeing dad standing by the window just looking out onto the street, even more withdrawn than usual, and I knew that he was worried for me; that my illness was serious. What used to happen was that I'd get delirious and have minor hallucinations. I'd look at my hand and think I could see my fingers swelling, then I'd start crying, telling mum and dad that I had fingers like sausages.

That was a sign to them. They knew as soon as I began talking about fingers like sausages that I was delirious and they'd call out the doctor, who'd do something to keep my temperature down and ask me, 'Do your fingers still look like sausages, Sally?'

'No, they're not now. They don't look like sausages now.'

Once, I awoke in the middle of the night. I was sleeping at the top of the bunk bed which was in my parents' room. Lying there, my eyes snapped open and I saw something. There, on the ceiling above my bed, was the image of a man's face.

It was as though it was projected onto the wallpaper, like a film running. Just his face; the image seemed to dissolve at his shoulders. He had long hair and a beard, which was a reddish colour. And he had blue eyes – the most piercing blue eyes.

'Hello, Sally,' he said. The voice was in my head; the image never altered, his mouth didn't move.

'Hello,' I whispered, thrilled he knew my name; comforted by that and by his voice.

'Sally, your fingers will never be sausages again,' he said.

'Really?' I whispered.

And my dad woke, up snuffling, saying, 'Sally? What's going on? Who you talking to? You all right?' His voice was thick with sleep.

There was a guard rail on the side of the bunk, to stop you falling out. I rolled onto my side and looked through it at my dad, who was sitting up in the double bed below me.

'There was a man on the ceiling,' I said. Dad's eyes instantly went there, seeing nothing. Well, cracks in the plaster, the odd cobweb, but not a man. 'He told me my fingers will never be sausages again.'

'Do you want a drink?' croaked dad, still groggy with sleep but looking worried now. 'Shall I wake your mother?'

'No,' I said, rolling onto my back, feeling calm and at peace. 'No, that's okay.'

'Go back to sleep,' he growled, and moments later I heard him snoring.

I looked back at the ceiling, willing the image to reappear, and it did, only now it had gained more shape. It had become three-dimensional, as though reaching out from the ceiling to touch me.

'Who are you?' I asked him, whispering.

'I've got to go now, Sally,' he said.

'Oh no,' I whispered, 'please don't go. Can't you talk to me a bit longer?'

'No, Sally.'

'Well, when will I see you again?'

'Not for a long time, Sally,' he told me. 'You won't see me for a very long time.'

He was gone. I lay for a moment, trying the same trick, attempting to will him back on to my ceiling. But he didn't return. All there was up there were cracks in the plaster and cobwebs. I turned on my side and went back to sleep.

Then, about a year later, my Auntie Maureen was getting married in the big church in the Fulham Road, the big Catholic church, so it was a full mass. I was a bridesmaid, but instead of being given flowers to hold, we clutched little books of prayer as we followed the bride up the aisle. After the vows, the bride and groom disappeared off to do their bride and groom things, and we brides-maids lined up along the front, waiting quietly for them to reappear, the only sound in church being the occasional cough or somebody clearing their throat. I looked down at the book of prayer I'd been given to hold, all tied up in a bit of ribbon, with a flower on the front.

Then I said, 'Oh.'

It was a picture on the back cover of the prayer book. It was him, the man on my ceiling.

'It's him,' I said.

The packed church looked back at me, eyebrows rais-ing. I looked up and towards mum and dad, who were already shifting in their seats, looking uncomfortable, their expressions saying, *What the bloody hell are you doing, Sally?*

But it was him, and I broke line. My dad's eyes widened in horror as I walked from my place to the pew where they sat.

'*What* are you doing?' growled dad in a whisper.

'Sally,' hissed mum, leaning over, 'get back there.'

Heads were turned our way.

'But it's him,' I said to my dad, holding out the prayer book towards him. 'That's that man who said my fingers wouldn't be sausages anymore.'

We'd never spoken about it. The morning we woke up nothing had been said about the man on my ceiling. But I'd woken up better, and I hadn't suffered hallucinations since; my fingers hadn't looked like sausages, and never would again.

Mum was smiling at curious members of the congregation as though to say, 'Typical. Tsk. Kids, eh?' then she bent across to speak to me.

'What are you on about? Pat, what's she talking about?'

'Get back over there,' said my dad to me, his face reddening.

And he was getting angry. Furious. And I didn't want that because, oh God, I did not want to make my dad angry. I'd wet my knickers. *Literally* wet my knickers. He frightened me that much.

I remember at dinner times we'd be sitting in our dark basement having dinner. He didn't like a lot of talking. He didn't like chatter. I've always been a chatterbox, so every now and then I'd get that terrifying look: 'You sit at the table to *eat*, not talk,' he'd bark. Either that or I'd get the handle of a knife across my knuckles. We were always made to eat all our dinner – I suppose everyone was back then – but thanks to that there's so much food I can't stomach as an adult. Bread and butter. I hate it, can't eat it. I can't bear the smell because it reminds me of the basement at Waldemar. And lamb, too. It was such a tiny room, the smell of the cooking just clung to you. The smell of lamb now takes me back to that dark room, to the look my dad gave me to make me shut up, when I knew I better had, or else.

The same look he was giving me now; the look that froze the blood.

'Get back over there,' he whispered darkly. And I didn't need telling again.

I scooted back to the line and stood with my head

bowed, the church settling back into silence around me. Just a few embarrassed coughs.

But I was upset and already sniffling as we filed out of the church. By the time it came to photographs I was in floods of tears, and my mum had to come over and say, 'Come on, what you up to? They want you for the pictures. What's the matter?'

Dad came over. They stood towering over me. They both smoked; had lit up as soon as we got out of the church.

'What's up with you?' said my mother.

'It's the man,' I said, pointing at my prayer book. 'It's the man I saw on the ceiling.'

'What man on the ceiling?' She turned to dad: 'What's she going on about?'

'Oh that,' he said. 'That was nothing, something she said last year. I dunno, some man on the ceiling who said something to her.'

Turning her attention back to me, she pulled the prayer book out of my hands and stared at it for a second or so. 'This is the man you saw on the ceiling?' she said.

'Yes,' I replied.

She thrust the book under my father's nose. 'That's Jesus. She's seen Jesus on the ceiling.'

'Bloody hell,' said my dad.

The man in the picture was Jesus as portrayed in a painting called 'The Light of the World' by William Holman Hunt, painted in 1854. It shows Jesus holding a lantern and wearing a crown of thorns, which the man on the ceiling wasn't. But the beard, the hair, the eyes — they were his.

He'd told me I wouldn't see him again for a very long time, and growing up I never quite worked out what he meant. It was only as I got older that I worked it out. He'll be there for me when I die, I'm sure of it.

Eight

Do you remember a character called Martha Longhurst on *Coronation Street*? She always wore a beret and glasses. How I smiled when I first saw her on television. She reminded me so much of Little Peg.

Little Peg was an old lady, a friend of Nanny Gladys who never really stopped mourning her, just like my mum never did. She was known as Little Peg because, well, she was called Peg and she was so small. She'd never married. My nan used to take care of her, giving her a little money every now and then, and I suppose you could say Little Peg was a bit lost without her. So she used to visit us at Waldemar Avenue, because it reminded her of Nan. She'd arrive wearing her trenchcoat and beret then sit downstairs with us and mum would give her cups of tea. But she was ill, we were told, and had to have her own cup. Mum had set one aside for her and she used to warn us about it.

'That's Little Peg's cup,' she told us sternly. 'She's had TB. You're not to touch that.' You can't catch TB off a cup as far as I know, but there were all kinds of old wives' tales flying about in those days.

Then Little Peg went to the sanatorium for a while, and when she came out she was well again.

'This,' said my mum, holding Little Peg's special cup

and saucer, 'is going in the bin.' She smiled at Little Peg, who sat at the kitchen table in her knitted beret and glasses. 'You can drink out of our cups now, love,' she said, and threw the old cup and saucer away.

For the first time, Little Peg drank out of our cups and saucers, which was wonderful. Later, when she got up to leave, I watched her go, seeing something on her – something on her back.

Mum returned from seeing her off.

'What was that big bit of paint on Peg's coat?' I asked.

'What bit of paint? There wasn't a mark on her.'

'Down her back. There was a big black mark down her back.'

My mother looked at me oddly, as though wanting to say, 'What are we going to do with you?' but thinking better of it.

The next thing we heard, Little Peg had got the TB again. She didn't come back to the basement after that. Tuberculosis, the disease of the lungs, like a black mark on them, had claimed her.

'Bloody hell,' said my mother when we found out, looking at me strangely. 'And you know what, she drank out of our cups that day.'

I sat there, looking at her, and she continued to give me this odd look, as though trying to make sense of me.

They were so new to me, these visions, sensations – whatever you called them. I was just a little girl and I'd say that on average something would happen once a fortnight. Something I was just too young to fully under-stand or control. I'd blurt out a strange observation, hear or see odd happenings at Waldemar Avenue, and when I said things, I did so without thinking about them; they'd just appear, surprising me as much as the person they were directed at. Looking back, it was as though I'd been given a great gift, but there was no instruction manual. I was having to work things out for myself, learning the hard way . . .

'What did you say?' barked Mr Flat one day, steam virtually shooting out of his ears.

He'd just told the class that his two sons were due to visit and help us with our reading, when I piped up, 'Their schools must cost you a lot of money.'

One of my out-of-nowhere knowings. A sudden flash of knowledge that appeared before I knew it. It surprised me almost as much as it did him. And it surprised him a lot.

'What did you say?' he repeated. His eyes were wide behind his specs; his bushy eyebrows bunching together.

'I just said . . .' I began.

'Don't you ever talk about my family again,' he said, spraying spit at me. '*Never* talk about my family again.'

He made me stand on a chair in the middle of the hall for that. Almost all day he made me stand on the chair, until another teacher told him I should come done now; I'd been up there for long enough. And then, just for good measure, Mr Flat made me stand on the chair some more. And the whole time I stood on that chair I cried and clenched my fists with frustration. It just wasn't fair. It was not fair. All I'd done was say something. Something that was true. I knew it to be true. Why was I in trouble? How could that be wrong?

What he said, at the end of the day when he finally let me off the chair, was, 'I'll forget about this if you forget about it.' So I did. I told nobody. Why, I wondered, did it matter where Mr Flat's children went to school? Only later, growing up, did I become aware that it was one of those 'touchy' subjects people like to keep quiet about.

Another teacher, called Mr Jenkins, had a plimsoll he used for discipline. He'd even given it a name, Charlie, and one day he came at a classmate with it. I remember it so well. There was a fire in the classroom. Imagine that. And it roared away, and here was Mr Jenkins, brandishing Charlie, about to use it on the boy sitting next to me.

I blurted out, 'You're only going to hit him because of your wife.'

Mr Jenkins stopped like he'd run into an invisible wall. Beside me, the boy about to receive Charlie cowered, waiting for the blow that didn't come.

'What did you say?'

What did you say? Oh my gawd, how many times did I hear that from adults as I was growing up?

'I said you're only going to do that because you got angry with your wife this morning and you threw a cup at her.'

His eyes widened. Slowly, he lowered Charlie.

'It was a yellow cup,' I continued, breathlessly, the words tumbling out of me, 'and it had black spots on it.'

Now his mouth dropped open, then began to work up and down as though he wanted to say something but couldn't find the words. He reddened, the veins in his neck were going, *boom, boom, boom,* and finally he found the words: 'You wicked, wicked girl,' he roared. 'Get out. Get out of my classroom now.'

He sent me out to stand in the hall, where the head-master found me and asked what was wrong. He knew, I think. He understood. And he believed me, too, when I told him what I'd seen. After lunch I was allowed back in class, but Mr Jenkins wouldn't look at me. He never once looked me in the eye again, the whole time I was at that school. Later, my mum found out about the incident, I think at a parents' evening, and when she got back that night she took me by the shoulders. 'Sally, if you see things like that again, you just keep them to yourself, all right?'

I wasn't the only one who saw things, though. Well, not at Waldemar Avenue, anyway. My Uncle Derek married a woman called Rita and they came back to live at Walde-mar. They were in the top flat, the one Mrs and Mrs Abel used to have, and one day Rita came running down the stairs, all in a flap. She'd seen something in the flat, she insisted. A ghost, she said, her face as white as one. She'd been in the flat and seen a woman walk around the bed, wearing a cardigan, her sleeves rolled up. Standing frozen with fear, Rita had watched as the woman walked around the bed, then out of the door. Next she heard footsteps on the stairs and had dashed out to look, but seen nothing.

'What was she wearing again?' said my mum sharply.

But I knew. From the moment Rita had described her,

I knew the woman was Nanny Gladys, who had always worn her sleeves rolled up. She was fanatical about it. I'm the same myself, funnily enough.

So other people did sometimes see them as well, I thought, watching as mum tried to calm Rita down. She was shaking, drained of colour. Other people could see them, too, but it was different for them. They were frightened of the spirits that lived in Waldemar. But I wasn't.

To me, those spirits were part of the house. I felt almost as though I belonged to them, and that they would protect me: from getting burnt on the iron, from catching a chill and from seeing fingers like sausages. I had nothing to fear from them. Not from dead people. It was the living who scared me.

Like the woman at Munster Road School. She was a helper, really, a monitor. But she had it in for Gina and me. It's not the kind of thing you're really aware of as a child: the fact that an adult doesn't like you, but you don't need to be a psychic to sense it. Much, much later I learnt that this woman had problems with our family.

She was helping with art class one day, a lesson held way up high at Munster Road, in the attic space. Art equipment was kept in the eaves either side of the room and one day I sensed something in there, a presence, and crawled inside.

Instantly, I felt cosy and comfortable. The sort of feeling you get when you're among good friends. I knew straight away I wanted to stay in the eaves, and that I might have a new friend to play with.

It was so warm. So, so warm.

'What are you doing in there?'

It was her. Her head was in the little doorway to the eaves and she stared down the passage at me, mouth in a straight line of disapproval.

I pushed myself further back into the darkness, not wanting to leave.

'Come on,' she snapped, 'I haven't got all day.'

'I'm not coming out,' I said.

'Yes, you are. Get out here now.'

Tell her you were born on a bus, a voice told me. A voice from my friend in the eaves. The spirit wanted me to taunt her.

'I'm not coming out,' I told her. 'And anyway, I don't like, you, because I was born on a bus.'

Even in the gloom I could see her face redden. '"Born on a bus"? You weren't born on a bus, you bloody little cow. I know all about you and your mother.'

'You don't know anything about my mother . . .'

Say it again. Tell her you were born on a bus.

'. . . I was born on a bus.'

'You're just like her. You're just like her. I know all about her.'

And with that she reached into the eaves and dragged me out. As she did I said a silent farewell to my friend and thanked him or her. Instead of being angry at being pulled from my hiding place, I felt elated. The woman couldn't hurt me. Not when I had forces looking out for me.

Nine

Something happened one day when I was out guying. Now I'm really showing my age: back then, to celebrate Guy Fawkes' Night, we would make a guy (a stuffed figure dressed in old clothes), then take him out in an old go-kart or pram and ask passers-by for a penny for the guy. I can't remember the last time I saw kids doing it, but we never missed a year when we were growing up. Same guy, every year. The guy was supposed to be put on a bonfire, but we kept ours; he'd get put in the cellar ready for next year. His head was an upside-down, empty Chianti bottle, one of those huge, bulbous bottles with its base covered in straw. Dad had done it for us – he was so clever like that. And what I'd do, I'd take my guy across the road, by which I mean Fulham Road, up to where there were some posh houses, hoping to get some extra money.

I was sitting there one day on the street, my guy lying at my side with his Chianti-bottle head lolling, when a man appeared before me.

'Penny for the guy?' I asked him.

He looked at me. He wore work clothes but I don't remember exactly what. What I do remember is him bending towards me, and at that moment I had the strangest feeling of *I know you*, the same sensation I often experienced seeing spirits.

Except this man wasn't a spirit. He may have been a ghost, of sorts. But he wasn't a spirit. He was a stranger, a passer-by. I didn't recognize him, yet the feeling that I somehow knew him was so overpowering I heard myself say, 'Oh, hello,' the greeting bright and cheerful, the way you might greet a family friend or teacher.

He regarded me. 'What are you doing?'

'I'm sorry?' I said.

'What are you doing *here*,' he said, 'What are you doing on this side of the road?' He gestured behind himself across Fulham Road, at the junction with Waldemar Avenue, and again I had a powerful sense that we knew one another; that he knew where I lived – and it wasn't strange or uncomfortable. I didn't feel threatened. It seemed like the most natural thing in the world.

Now he said, 'Where's Gina?'

I didn't know.

'At home, I think,' I replied.

'Is she with your mother? Is she with Beryl?'

'Yes.'

'So what are you doing out here by yourself?'

'I'm guying,' I said, then, 'I'm sorry.'

I could see that I had done something wrong. It was in his eyes.

'I'm just guying,' I repeated and then it came out. It blurted out. A question that seemed to come from nowhere.

I said, 'Where have you been?'

It happens so often. So much of what I do bypasses the normal Sally-mind. Often the first I know of it is when I say it. Growing up, it would get me into so much trouble, you wouldn't believe. It was about to get me into trouble again.

He looked taken aback for a moment and straightened a little as though trying to read my face.

'Don't worry,' he said, 'I see you often.' And he reached toward me, holding out his hand and dropping five shillings into my palm. 'Now I want you to go home to your mother and tell her that your father says you're not to go over the other side of the road guying, and that he gave you five shillings. All right?'

I did as he said, skipping home, happy with my five shillings. I either thought nothing of what he'd said – that it was just one of those things adults say – or my young mind blocked it out. Who knows? Perhaps if I had given it a bit of thought, I wouldn't have done what I did next. Dumping my guy by the front door, I skipped right into the house, down into the basement and told my mum exactly what had just happened.

'What?'

She took the stairs four at a time. She was furious.

I dashed up after her to see the front door swinging open on its hinges, and ran out into the street.

She was fast, my mum. When she was younger, 15 or 16, she was a runner, a sprinter, and ran for the county. By the time I'd got up the stairs and out into the street, she was at the end of it, standing at the junction of Fulham Road with her hands on her hips, looking this way and that. She stood there for a moment or so, then turned around and came marching back towards home.

'I'll kill him,' she seethed, striding right past me and into the front door. 'I'll bloody kill him.'

I remained on the street for a moment or so, recovering in her furious wake. She was like a force of nature; a beautiful force of nature. She looked like Elizabeth Taylor when she was younger. Can you imagine that? An athletic Liz Taylor look-alike. The double of Liz Taylor they used to say. No wonder the men used to flock around her when she was younger. Gorgeous, she was, always up for a laugh, loved her parties, liked to flirt. She could charm the birds out of the trees.

She was strict with us girls but always loving. I remember she always liked to brush our hair. I mean, we were like little dolls to her; when we were small she used to dress us in matching outfits, so doing our hair was just another part of that. She'd brush it and plait it, do it in different styles each day. She used to tie it in ribbons and a childhood image I'll always carry is of the clotheshorse, an old wooden one, with our different hair ribbons drying on it: all different colours, polka dot and stripes. Funny the things you remember, isn't it? She used to hold tresses of hair in her mouth, clenching them in bared teeth, ignoring our squeals as she tied the ribbons. If our squeals got too loud, we'd get a hit with the brush, the bristles side, which left a cluster of blood spots on our shoulders. As an adult I look back on the hair-brushing, even the whack with the brush, and I smile. We never got affection from dad; it all came from mum and there's something wonderful about your mum brushing your hair; something that makes you think she'll love you for ever.

But there was another side to her, even more fierce, and every now and then I'd see it. Whenever we used to walk past a certain doctor's surgery, she'd spit on the doorstep.

'Why'd you do that, mummy?' I asked her one day.

'Because that's where the bastard who killed my mother works,' she hissed.

Ten

Growing up, we weren't bought toys the way kids are nowadays (and listen to me, *still* going on about the good old days), although occasionally my dad brought us gifts from Petticoat Lane. He'd go every Sunday, disappearing early in the morning, then returning late at night, having traded birds in the pubs round the market. He brought us hula hoops one day and we almost instantly abandoned our huge skipping rope (which was really a few skipping ropes tied together) in favour of this new fad, which we practised day and night. If there had been a cup for hula-hoop champion of Waldemar Avenue, it would have gone to me, I'm telling you. I was tiny back then and I would have one hula hoop around my neck, another around my waist, one around my knees. I can remember Barbara and Pamela's mum coming over to ours and asking dad if he could get the girls hula hoops the next time he went to Petticoat Lane; he bought them for nearly the entire street in the end. Oh, and I also remember him coming home with Davey Crockett hats one Sunday too, but that was very much it.

The only other time we were given toys or presents was on our birthdays. The birthdays were great, they really were. You know how my mum liked to hold a party? Well, birthdays were an excuse to do just that, and we'd often end up hosting them at Waldemar, even if they weren't ours. Mum had these rabbit moulds that she'd used for years and she'd make a blancmange in one and a jelly in the other. She'd use different flavours for the blancmange rabbit – pink along the bottom and chocolate on top. Oh, I loved chocolate blancmange, and still do, even to this day. She'd make fairy cakes, too. Sometimes, she'd make a birthday cake with rock-hard icing and our name on it. To see a cake with your name on was just the most amazing thing, it really was.

But you know what? We didn't get sacks and sacks full of presents on our birthdays. Not like ... well, I won't say it. We were never spoiled, that was the thing. We'd get one present from our parents – my roller skates really stick in my mind. At Easter we would get a few eggs from aunties and uncles, so we had a bit more then. No, Christmas was the thing. On Christmas morning, I would wake up, my heart sinking because the first job would be clearing the ice off the inside of the windowpane (we didn't have central heating). I'd have to hop out of my nice, warm bed – we used to wear bedsocks and cardigans, and snuggle up with hot-water bottles – and scrape off the ice, then quickly get back into bed. But one Christmas I awoke feeling something heavy on my toes, hearing the rustling of paper as I moved around. Instead of icy windows I was greeted by the sight of a pillowcase at the bottom of my bed, resting against my feet, full of presents. I can remember jumping on my mum's bed to wake her up, so we could open our pillowcases. In the bottom were nuts and a piece of coal for luck, plus a tangerine.

There were colouring pencils and – *oh* – a paint-by-numbers set.

Some other presents arrived for us that Christmas. Mum put them straight into the dustbin.

Another time, when we were much younger, I recall my mum saying, 'Father Christmas has been in the hall, go and look in the hall,' and we both shot through to the hall to see two prams, each with a dolly inside. One was dressed in pink and one in blue; our whole childhood was pink and blue. Mum would buy us exactly the same, but one in pink and one in blue. I always got the blue but wanted the pink.

Another year, I really, really wanted a radio and I got a red one, which I'll never, ever forget. I was one of those kids who used to listen to the radio under the bedclothes at night, tuning into Radio Luxembourg and all the pirate stations. By then me and my sister were in our own room, and I was sleeping on the bottom bunk, burrowing under the covers, tuning my radio. I liked hearing the crackle, enjoyed very, very carefully twiddling the tuning knob until out of the crackle I'd hear voices, music. Not so different to what I do now, really, only it's people I'm tuning into, not the radio. Gina used to complain from the top bunk. She used to say the radio was keeping her awake and I'd have to turn it down, holding it even closer to my ear to hear properly.

The year after that, I got a record player. Oh, that was absolutely incredible. A record player! We were growing up, you see. The 1950s had turned into the 1960s, and we were discovering pop music. Growing up, I lived for my music. I liked them all: The Beatles, The Rolling Stones, The Animals. I went to see The Beatles at Hammersmith Odeon in 1964, the first time Gina and I were allowed to go 'into town' on a bus. We went with a friend, and oh my gawd, the screaming. We all screamed our lungs out that night. Me for John: he was always my favourite. I remember waving a scarf at them. They were hardly bigger than dots, really, standing in front of this huge curtain.

And that was it for me. Pop music was it. We were always what you'd call latchkey kids, and I grew up running down into the basement to watch *The Flintstones* or *Popeye*, and running into my room for my record player and precious stack of vinyl.

On Saturdays we went to the cinema – the Regal at Walham Green. You had to be nine if you wanted to sit in the circle, otherwise you had to sit in the stalls and I remember being cross when I reached nine because I still had to sit in the stalls to keep my sister company. We liked *The Lone Ranger* and *The Dead End Kids*. By the age of 14 I was still going to the cinema, but this time it wasn't with my sister, it was with boys.

We'd gone from Munster Road School to St Marks, my secondary school, where I was one of the first 33 girls. As little girls going to Munster Road, mum used to dress us and do our hair every morning. As young ladies of St Marks, we had a uniform, so that stopped. We used to have to get ourselves ready and we'd lie in bed until dad appeared, tipping up the bed. There was no lazing around in bed with my dad around. Ouch. And I'm going to sound like a right old woman here, but I've absolutely no doubt that the values I have now, my whole work ethic, were instilled in me at that early age, on those cold mornings at Waldemar Avenue. It was strict – there was no doubt we had a strict upbringing. But it's served me well in life. None of us has ever used the system, the family has never ever been on income support, and I'm proud of that. I'm a socialist; I'll always vote Labour because I believe in helping the underdog. But even so, I was brought up in a family where you never asked for a handout: you got out there and you worked every day.

There was a gang of us who used to hang around together at St Marks. I used to do my 'thing' with them, they called it, where I'd just seem to 'know' something, or was able to tell what they were thinking. Often, I'd look at a photograph and be able to say something about the person pictured: 'Oh, she wants to be a policewoman,' something like that. Sometimes, I'd see the person in my head, all decked out in a policeman's uniform; sometimes it would just trip from my mouth before I had a chance to stop it. Most of the time – and here's when I used to think about Nanny Gladys and her tips to the City gents – I'd hardly even know I said it. I'd tell a friend something and then instantly forget it.

But when I blurted out something at home, mum's friends would say, 'Your Sally's a nosy little one, isn't she?' looking at me sideways. My mum laughing in reply, would say, 'Oh, yes, she does love looking in drawers, don't you, Sal?', or: 'Oh, she's got quite an imagination on her.' I'd feel confused, because I don't like looking in drawers. Believe me, it's quite the reverse.

But afterwards, walking away, mum would tell me, 'You're just like my mum, you are.' And do you know what? There was a note of pride in her voice. Maybe she wanted to protect me from other people with her little fibs about looking in drawers and how I had an over-active imagination, but really it just made her think of Nanny Gladys. That's what I like to think these days. Even so, she was always trying to find ways of explaining what I did. That they were my 'dreams' was the favourite one. And I quickly worked out that if I wanted my mum to listen to what I had to say, it was best to tell her I'd had another one of 'my dreams'. Then she'd want to listen.

Most of the time, though, people put it down to me having too much to say for myself. I remember my dad always used to say to me, 'You've got too much of what the cat licks its arse with, my girl.'

Charming.

Perhaps it was because of my psychic intuition that my mother treated me the way she did – talking to me as though I was an adult.

'What would you say,' she asked me one day, 'if I told you I'd been married before?'

We were standing in the kitchen at the time.

'Have you been married before, then?' I asked.

She just looked at me.

'Does that mean daddy's not my daddy?' I pressed. And I have no idea why I asked that question.

But I'll never forget the look on my mum's face when I did. It seemed to fall, her mouth moving as though unsure what to say next.

'Oh,' she said, her mind working, trying to think on her feet, 'he's your dad, but he's not Gina's dad, that's what it is, love.'

'Oh.'

Another day, we were sitting on a bed, looking at photographs from a box and one in particular jumped out at me, drawing a gasp as I studied it, because I suddenly had the most powerful sense that I was looking at the image from my dream.

'What's this?' I asked mum, showing her the photo. 'I know this.'

She took the picture from me.

'Oh, this,' she said. 'This is a picture I took of you on the iron bridge.'

I told her about the dream I used to have, the one where I felt I was constricted ('It's because you were strapped into the pram, Sal.') and how somebody would be calling my name but I was thinking, *That's not my name. Why are they calling me Sally when that's not my name.*

'Where were we going?' I asked. 'What were we doing?'

We sat on the bed, my feet swinging. Mum looked at me a long time, seeing what, I don't know. The Witch of Fulham, perhaps.

And she told me. She told me how each day she used to walk from Earlsfield to Fulham – miles, it was – across an iron bridge, to be with her mum. One day she stopped to take a picture, and that was it. This photograph of me in the pram, my face turned away from the camera slightly, the River Thames in the background. That picture. That exact moment. Somehow it became part of me, part of my psychic make-up.

'Someone was calling my name, but it wasn't my name.'

'Oh, Sal,' said my mum, and she told me that when I was first born I wasn't called Sally, my name was Michelle. But guess what? Old Nanny Gladys had a thing or two to say about that. Michelle was a foreign name, she said. It sounded French. (She wasn't a fan of the French, apparently. She may have been PC ahead of her time when it came to gay Uncle Tom, but that tolerance didn't extend to the French.) No, it would have to change. No granddaughter of hers was wandering around with a bleedin' French name. What about Sally?

She was a fan of Gracie Fields, you see, and at the time Gracie Fields' best-known song was 'Sally', so that's how I got my name.

My surname was West. And I suppose it was about then that I started learning about the other man in my mum's life, this 'Westy' she used to talk about – sometimes in quite graphic detail.

But it was a violent, volatile relationship. He used to beat her up. He'd strip her naked and kick her under the table. Once, she was washing nappies and this Westy came up behind her, took hold of her hair and rammed her face into the tap, breaking her nose. His name was Derek. Derek West. Over the years it came out. Mum had been married before, to Derek West, and they'd lived in Earlsfield together. She escaped to Waldemar Avenue, where she'd often stay the night to escape his fists. There would even be confrontations between Derek West and

Nanny Gladys at the door. He met his match there, don't you worry about that.

'Get out of it, you. I know what you've been up to. *Get out of it.*'

Eventually, mum left Derek West and Earlsfield for good and returned to Waldemar, where she resumed a relationship with Pat Thatcher, who had always been on the scene. He and Derek West had both been competing for my mother's affections. Derek had won, albeit only temporarily. So when mum and Derek split up, Pat came back on the scene.

Mum told me all of these stories as a child, talking as though I was an adult friend, not her daughter. Growing up, I was confused. I was confused about the visions and feelings I kept getting. The 'knowings'. Plus, I was confused about my mum and this Westy man, the fact that my surname was his and not my dad's. Why wasn't I a Thatcher?

At nine or ten the other kids in the playground would say, 'Oi, Westy, how come you're called Westy and yer mum's called Thatcher?'

'I dunno.'

'You ain't got a dad, that's why. Westy ain't got a dad.'

Later that night, I told my mum what they'd been saying at school.

'They say I ain't got a dad. Who's my dad?'

'You don't want to worry about that, love. Your dad's your dad, of course.'

'But you said . . .'

'Oh, don't you go bothering yourself with things I said

when you was little. You know what it's like? You just say things, don't you? Because you don't know what else to say.'

A few years later, as a teenager, I asked my dad, 'Are you my real dad?'

He glared at me. 'I don't want to talk about that he said,' and the subject was closed.

I used to wonder, *Why is it that I seem to know so much about other people, but so little about myself?*

Eleven

Walking with my mum towards Kelvedon Hall, I felt important, grown-up. Mum had been going to Spiritualist meetings – she went to try and contact Nanny Gladys – but usually she went alone or with a friend. Never with Gina or me; we were always in bed. This was different.

'You're coming with me tonight,' she'd told me that morning. We're going along to the circle at Kelvedon Hall. Joseph Benjamin will be there.'

Not that I knew the name then, but Joseph Benjamin was a well-known medium based in the area. He'd hold these Spiritualist 'circles', as they called them. After I got home from school that day I had something to eat and watched telly until mum came home.

'Right, come on then,' she said a bit later on, 'let's go,' and I leapt up, almost unable to believe that, for the first time, I was going out with mum. A 15-minute walk later and we arrived at the hall, a brick-built building at the side of an old convent, which was used as a school during the daytime and as a meeting room at night. We walked through blue entrance doors and into the hall; I was so excited.

And my heart sank.

At the back was a kitchen, separated from the main room by a serving counter with an urn steaming on it.

Around the sides were stacks of chairs put away after school. A few remaining chairs had been formed into a circle in the centre of the room and sitting in them were people holding cups and saucers, most of whom stopped mid-slurp to stare at me as I walked in, chatter evaporating as I made my entrance. Oh no, I thought, They're so *old*.

What had I expected? A bunch of Beatles fans? I don't know. People my mum's age perhaps (she was the second-youngest there), a bit more laughter and fun. You know what flashed through my mind? *Oh, they're so uncool.* You can't blame me, I was 15 and like every other 15-year-old I wanted to be older, but not quite *this* old, thank you very much.

Plus, they were all staring at me as if I was another species. I was, I quickly realized, with a sudden, embarrassed twinge, the guest of honour, the centre of attention. Mum hadn't told me that on the way. 'Oh, it's a circle,' she'd assured me, 'you're just going to sit in on it.' But the centre of attention? Again, at 15, it's not what you really want, is it?

A man stood up from the circle as we clip-clopped over the wooden floor towards the group. This was Joseph Benjamin. Like the rest of them, he seemed impossibly ancient. He was going bald on top, wore glasses, a sober black suit and a white shirt. He greeted me, introduced me to the other members of the circle – six of them, a mix of men and women – and offered me his seat, which I took. Then he nodded to my mother, who left.

Why she left I'm not quite sure. Perhaps it was felt her presence would disrupt the circle – affect what would turn out to be my test. Off she went, though, closing the Kelvedon Hall door behind herself with a clunk. I felt an immediate sense of trust with Joseph Benjamin but even so, I wasn't sure about mum going. I watched the door shut, then turned my attention to the circle of people, who all smiled at me. Pleasant, but expectant smiles. I smiled back, and the circle began.

'Sally,' said Mr Benjamin, 'we're going to open ourselves to spirit world. Is that okay with you?'

I nodded, not really sure that it was. He walked around the circle. The spiritualists took deep breaths and rested their hands in their laps, straight-backed. Some closed their eyes. Others stared right at me, their gaze making me squirm, making me feel like I was on show and under glass. With them all assuming positions like this, it all looked terribly formal. I sat wondering if I was supposed to do the same.

Then Mr Benjamin, now standing at my shoulder, said, 'Let's begin then. Sally?'

I turned my head and looked back at him, grateful for something to look at that wasn't the rest of the circle. 'Yes?'

'If I point at Joan, why don't you tell me what you see?' He indicated a woman opposite. 'What can you see?'

And there was somebody there, I saw. A man. At her shoulder. A man in spirit.

'I can see a man,' I said, craning round to look up at Mr Benjamin. 'Is that right?'

'Yes, that's fine,' he said, 'but look at Joan, Sally, don't look at me. Is he still there?'

He was.

'Yes,' I said, not taking my eyes off him. He was almost solid, like the little girl's grandpa, but not quite, as though slightly hazy at the edges.

I described him to the group. 'Oh, and he's her husband,' I finished. That information had just come to me, popped into my head.

Opposite me, Joan took a sharp intake of breath.

'Is he saying anything?' asked Mr Benjamin.

'Yes,' I said. 'I can't hear him properly, but he's saying something about love.'

'Joan, has Sally described Bill?'

Joan dabbed at her eyes, sniffing slightly and nodding.

Mr Benjamin walked around the circle, talking to a man. 'Graham, look at Sally, what do you see?'

'I see her aura,' said Graham, 'She has an orange aura.'

It was all I could do not to laugh. I imagined myself looking like one of the children on a Ready Brek packet.

Then I thought, *Why can't I see an aura? Perhaps I'm supposed to see one of those. Perhaps I'm supposed to be sitting with my hands in my lap, closing my eyes and looking for Ready Brek kids.*

Somebody else was asked to look at me and say what they saw. But nothing they said made any sense, and I began to get the feeling that some of those in the circle couldn't do what I did. That was it – that was what the closed eyes and serene expressions were all about. They were trying. They were trying to get it. And failing. Immediately, I felt different because I didn't have to try. I never had. These things, they just came to me.

And then I was being asked to do it again, seeing spirits standing with another member of the circle. It was coming easily to me. Everybody present had someone with them in spirit, they all did; the spirits stood at their shoulders and I could see each one. It was as though when I turned my attention to someone new their spirits would come into focus and the others faded slightly into the background.

It's the same when I'm on tour nowadays. Even if I'm looking at a thousand faces, I'm able to bring individual spirits into focus. I've got clever at it; I've had years of practice. I can phase spirits in and out. They're still there; I'm still aware of them, and they bring with them a kind of murmur, a hubbub that I have to try and tune in and out of, but over the years, I've learnt to bring them in and out of focus. There's a bit of an art to it. Not that I'd perfected it then, of course, I was still getting used to seeing so many spirits in one go. And I was seeing so many of them.

(Getting rid of them was another matter. Controlling them, still another matter.)

Over the hour, I even saw other spirits unconnected with the group – a lady walking along the side of the hall.

'Well done, Sally, very good,' said Mr Benjamin each time, still travelling the circle. I caught him looking at me a couple of times and felt like I was doing well for him. What I felt when he looked at me – and I remember this so well – is that we saw the same. He didn't respond to the others like that.

At the end of the session mum came to collect me, but before she did, Joseph Benjamin bent to talk to me.

'You are me,' he said. 'You will carry on my work.'

No, I thought, I won't be doing your work. I want to be a midwife. I certainly don't want to be hanging around in draughty halls with all these uncool people. But we were very well brought-up children, always said our pleases and thank yous, always asked to be excused from the dinner table. So I just smiled at Joseph Benjamin and nodded, and my mum took me home.

'Did it go well?' she enquired as we made our way back.

'No,' I fibbed. Well, it wasn't a great big lie. After all, for me it hadn't gone well. Frankly, I would rather have been at home mooning over John Lennon. It had gone well the way she meant, but no way did I want to go back. And thanks to me being economical with the truth that night, I didn't go back. To my mum, the little experiment had been a failure.

I didn't realize it then, being so keen not to return, but I learnt a lot that night – things that would takes years to fully sink in. 'You are me,' Joseph Benjamin had said. I think that was the night I began to understand what I was – what I could do.

Twelve

Gina got ill one day. And I don't know what it was – perhaps it was the spirits at Waldemar Avenue, or perhaps it was Grandma Brodie or Nanny Gladys watching over us – but I knew. Somehow I knew that she was going to die and I screeched it.

'She's going to die. Mummy, she's going to die. We've got to get an ambulance.'

And my mother looked at me, her mouth dropping open. 'Okay,' she said, 'We'll phone . . .'

It had started earlier. Gina was complaining of pains. She was lying on the sofa with her arms wrapped around her middle. Our new sofa. It was Ercol. I'd been with mum when she bought it and it had been delivered, taken downstairs to the basement where it took pride of place. Gina had been on it since morning. She'd woken up complaining of a tummy bug and she was in pain, obviously. Gina was always different to me growing up. She cried often, she had a different temperament, so we were used to seeing her in tears; she'd often be the one to cause a fuss. But this was different. Her eyes were shut tight, tears of pain squeezing out from beneath the eyelids. She was curled up on the sofa like she wanted to disappear into herself. She writhed with the pain.

Mum stayed off work. It must have been school holidays at the time, because I was at home too, and we skulked around the basement, me and mum, watching Gina moaning and holding her tummy on our new Ercol sofa.

That morning, a doctor came. We never had much luck with doctors, it seems. First Nanny Gladys, now this one telling us we shouldn't worry; that Gina just had a tummy bug. Mum seemed happier after he'd gone. Even after what had happened with Nanny Gladys she trusted what the doctor said. That's how ingrained it was in those days. You didn't ask for a second opinion. The doctor had said she'll be okay. The doctor said it was just a tummy bug.

Gina continued writhing on the couch. Her condition got worse after the doctor had left. She began vomiting and her temperature rose. I could see mum beginning to worry now, chewing her lip as she moved around the basement.

'Get the doctor out again,' I said, but I could see her mind working. She'd already called him out. He'd come and told us Gina just had a tummy bug. Plus, in our family we had this ethos: you don't call for the doctor until you really need him. By rights, you needed to be dying before you called out the doctor. I'd broken my finger and we didn't even bother the chemist. And we'd *already had* the doctor out. And he'd already said it was just a tummy bug, so we shouldn't really have called him out in the first place and what if he came again and still said it was a tummy bug? We'd have had him out twice for no good reason . . .

I didn't need to be psychic to know all this was going

through her head. It would have been going through the head of any mother in the 1960s.

'You've got to get the doctor out,' I said, standing at the arm of the sofa, watching Gina and seeing my mum pacing the room and chewing her lip.

'Wait a minute, Sal, wait a minute,' she said, and I could see all that indecision racing around behind her eyes.

On the sofa, Gina moaned and shifted, pulling her legs tighter into her chest.

'*Mum*,' I insisted, swinging back to look at mum, who had her hand to her mouth, her eyes wide with worry over the top of her fist.

And I saw it – no, I didn't see it. I *knew* it, as surely as I'd ever known anything. Gina was going to die. She was going to die unless we got the doctor out.

'You got to get him out,' I wailed.

'*Shh*, Sally.'

'*Gina's going to die*,' I shouted. 'I can see it. Gina's going to die unless we call out the doctor. I can see it.'

Mum looked at me. A quick look like, *Oh my God*. And I'm sure she knew; I'm sure she believed.

She must have done, because she left that second. I watched over Gina; she was vomiting bile by then. Mum returned and we waited for the doctor.

'Do you have a phone?' he asked, almost the moment he walked in, hardly needing to examine Gina.

No, we didn't have a phone. The doctor left and half an hour later an ambulance appeared; she was rushed into hospital and went straight into surgery. She was moments away from death, they told us.

It turned out she had peritonitis. It meant her appendix had burst. It had burst and according to a doctor at the hospital 'we opened her up and her insides were swimming with poison'.

After the operation she contracted pneumonia, and again it was touch and go. All I remember is, I wasn't allowed to see her for a week, only mum and dad were. They wouldn't let me come; I think they thought it was too frightening, because they really thought for a while there that Gina might die. She was on open order, you see, which meant she could die at any time. I remember my mum wailing, 'Oh my God, she's on open order, she's on open order.'

When at last I was allowed to see her, I was briefed: 'Gina can't talk, and you've got to be quiet, just hold her hand.'

But she'd been asking for me, Gina had. I can remember walking in to see her sitting upright on all these pillows with a big thick tube going up into her nose, and as I sat with her a nurse came into the room and told her she was going to draw off some poison, extracting a thick, green fluid from inside my sister.

She was in hospital three or four weeks. As she got better I was able to see more of her, although the conversations were a bit one-sided when I did: she'd lost her voice; couldn't speak for about two months. But when she did, she said, 'You saved my life, Sally.'

Thirteen

She was off school for so long time after that, Gina was. Meanwhile, I was coming to the end of my schooldays, still knocking around with the same old gang. Then came time to leave and although I'd had hopes of going onto further education it wasn't to be. These days kids get encouraged to follow a career path; they get advice on the best subjects to take, what grades they need, where to train and all that. Not when I was at school. You were on your own, mate.

Because I had this long-term desire to be a midwife when I grew up, I took sciences at school: biology and chemistry were the two I liked the best. The trouble was I was terrible at maths. Still am, actually. Things didn't go that well and I ended up leaving school with no qualifications.

I went home and looked in the paper picking out the most medical job I could find, which was working at Betty Roney's Trichology clinic at Welbeck Street. I got the job and that was it, as simple as that. I'd gone from being a schoolgirl to one of the hundreds of thousands of people who trekked into the centre of London each day, by bus and tube, car and bicycle. I was a worker now.

Trichology, just in case you don't know, is the treatment of the hair and scalp, so we saw a lot of clients with scalp problems: dandruff, thinning on top, that kind of thing. I remember my first day there. On arrival, Mrs Roney told me to go and collect my uniform from an outlet somewhere near Marylebone High Street. Now I don't know if you know London that well, but Welbeck Street and Harley Street are only a hop, skip and a jump away from Marylebone High Street. The thing was, I didn't know that then. I'd grown up in Fulham and very, very rarely strayed outside. This going to work thing was like a whole new world to me. So I got lost, didn't I? First day at work and she goes and gets lost. Typical.

Things improved, though. We had lots of celebrity clients, most of whom probably don't want it advertised that they were receiving treatment for baldness or dandruff, so I'll spare their blushes (just send a fiver to the usual address, you know who you are!), and I ended up shampooing the heads of pop stars, TV presenters, sportsmen, you name it.

Plus, it seemed like every lunchtime I'd bump into someone else famous. I remember going out to lunch and wandering along Welbeck Street and who should be coming towards me but Paul McCartney, with a girl with blonde hair. I ran back into the clinic, babbling to my friend Valerie: 'Oh my God, oh my God, I've just seen Paul McCartney. Paul McCartney!'

And her response was, 'Oh my God, oh my God, who was he with?'

'Oh my God,' I said, 'it wasn't Jane Asher.'

'Oh my God, oh my God.'

I don't suppose star-struck girls have changed much over the years.

Anyway, it definitely wasn't Jane Asher, so I described the girl he was with and the very next week it was in all the papers: Paul McCartney had a new photographer girlfriend called Linda. I must have been one of the first to see them together. Another time I saw Billy Fury. I was a bit of a gofer for Mrs Roney, really, and I was always running odd jobs, and there on the street one afternoon was Billy Fury, staring in a shop window, looking at some chess sets. *The* Billy Fury. Wow!

It was a wonderful time. I was growing up, but it felt like the world was growing up, too. Or at least the London bit of it was. It felt like the country was finally emerging out of the shadow of the war years.

I needed to earn a bit more, though, so after about a year at Betty Roney's clinic I found another job, this time as a dental nurse. Not only were the wages better, but it was at a surgery on North End Road, closer to home, so I could walk and not have to brave the tubes, which at that time were terrible; I'm sure they were worse then than they are now.

Brenners was the name of the surgery and I loved it. When I was there I found that I didn't have the psychic incidences I'd been getting as a younger child, perhaps because I was concentrating on improving my career, or maybe because I simply wasn't opened up the way I somehow was at Waldemar. Still, there would be the odd thing, of course. A spirit I saw in the basement, for example. There was a particular nurse at the surgery, an Australian, who went down to the basement to fetch something – we stored swabs, tissue and sundries there.

It was a big old room, and there was definitely a presence down there. A man. He must have been a strong presence, because she came up from the storeroom complaining about him, saying that she felt someone in there with her, and how it made her feel uncomfortable.

'Oh, that's because we've got a ghost down there,' I said breezily.

She hardly ever spoke to me again; barely even looked at me.

But I still wasn't used to it – that some people are scared of the spirits. It was around about the same time that we had another spirit at Waldemar and once again I was the only one not to be worried by it. This one was an angry guy who came at us through the record player that we used to keep in Uncle Derek's bedroom. My mother and I were in there at the time. Just us, a bed, wardrobe, fireplace and record player. I remember it quite clearly because I was moving to pick up a Cliff Richard record when we heard a voice coming through the record player.

'Shut that bloody racket up.'

We both froze. There was nobody in the house. Dad was at work. The voice had come through the record player and it wasn't muffled or distant either. It was as clear as a bell: *shut that bloody racket up.*

And yet again, I found myself completely at ease with the idea of the presence there; it just didn't bother me at all. I looked at the Cliff Richard cover in my hand. Fancy that, I thought, a spirit who doesn't like Cliff.

My mum, on the other hand: you should have seen her.

Running around the place, trying to find some explanation for the noise, peering at the record player. Completely spooked out by it.

To me, the spirit in that room had just as much right to be there as we did. The same went for the spirit in the storeroom at Brenners.

It was at Brenners that I met a great friend, Valerie Watts, and also while I was there that I went to visit the medium Doris Stokes. People often can't believe it that our paths crossed, but they did, even – if I'm absolutely honest – if it was a bit of an anti-climax.

Doris Stokes lived in the Chelsea/Wandsworth area. She was well-known then – this was in the mid-60s – but she wasn't famous the way she later became. That was in the late-70s, when she really became a bit of a household name. No, when I met her she was still doing readings from her flat in West London. It was all the idea of this friend from work, whose name I can't recall I'm afraid, but she made the appointment. It was going to cost £8.

The door to Doris Stokes' flat was opened by her husband, who ushered us into a kitchen to wait. When it came to my turn I went into the sitting room, as normal a sitting room as you could wish for. Two armchairs were placed either side of a fireplace, a rug on the floor between them. Sitting in one of the chairs, Doris indicated to me to sit opposite her which I did, getting my first good look at her. Immediately I found myself feeling at ease in her presence; it was like sitting with an auntie or grandma. She had white hair and a warm smile and wore a cardigan.

I introduced myself and we chatted for a moment or so, until she said, 'I can see you in a car.'

We didn't have a car. I couldn't even drive then; never even thought about having a car.

'Oh,' I said, slightly disappointed.

'It's a turquoise car,' she went on. 'And I can see the faces of two little girls, they're little blonde girls, they're looking out of the back window of the car, waving at you. Oh, how lovely, they're your daughters.'

Oh my gawd, I was thinking. I didn't even want kids then. The thought of having kids . . .

She told me who was with me in spirit, mentioning Nanny Gladys, but it was over very quickly and I remember thinking, *Oh, that didn't last long*, and wanting a bit more. What she'd said was accurate but I still wanted more.

Just as I was about to leave, I told her, 'I think I see things.'

'I know you do,' she said, nodding, 'I can see that in you.'

'I live in this house,' I went on. 'It's full of ghosts and spirits.'

'Yes, dearie,' she said, 'I know that, too.'

She smiled and I left. Later, she became world famous, but I can't say she had any major affect on me at the time. She said she recognized I had the same ability, but then all she did was agree with me; she may not have seen it. And what she told me, well, a lot of it I just didn't understand – I was too young to, really. Years later, we did have a turquoise car, though. I said to John, 'Oh, Doris Stokes predicted I'd have a car this colour.'

And of course, I did have daughters, but not two. I have three daughters, so who knows why Doris said just two. Either she got it wrong, or the spirit world was telling us something far too subtle for us to understand.

As I have already said, it wasn't a life-changing meeting, even though we both have so much in common. You've got to realize, at the time I was just enjoying being a teenager in the 1960s, which was probably the best time to be a teenager there's ever been. It's not like I was swanning down Carnaby Street in my hip and trendy gear – it was only really the rich kids who could afford all that; we had to make do with the cheaper copies – but I was young and into fashion and music . . .

And boys. And booze. I'd discovered sex and going out getting drunk on vodka and lime or Pernod, so believe it or not, the world of Doris Stokes and spiritualist circles was not one I wanted anything to do with. There was fun to be had.

And I had to go and ruin it by getting married, didn't I?

How? Well, put it this way, I must be the only person who's ever got married after an argument about eggs.

His name was Brian (actually, that isn't his real name, but let's just call him Brian), and he was my boyfriend at the time. Not a particularly special boyfriend. Not a boyfriend I was in love with. Just a guy I was seeing.

It was 1971. I was still at Waldemar Avenue then, the house continuing to exert its hold on me. I was working at Brenners, hanging around with Valerie Watts. On days off I'd either haunt clothes shops or hang out with boys. This particular afternoon – the day of the famous egg argument – Brian had come back to ours and we were downstairs in the basement, in the kitchen, where I cooked Brian an omelette, using three eggs.

Not long later, dad arrived home from work. As usual, I didn't get much of a greeting. The basement was always dark, but it seemed to get even gloomier when he was around. The atmosphere just changed.

And oh, how it changed on this particular day, because dad had come home wanting an egg for dinner. And I'd just used the last three.

'Who's used these eggs?' he said, staring right at me accusingly.

'I have,' I said. (Was I brave because Brian was sat there, witnessing my dad getting angry? Perhaps. Or maybe I'd just found my feet a little. Enough to stand up to him. I was a young woman now. The days of weeing my knickers were over.)

'*You silly cow,*' he barked. Oh my God, he was a quiet man, but when he went he really went. It was like standing in a wind tunnel, being buffeted by his fury.

'I've only made an omelette for my boyfriend,' I said.

Dad shot a filthy look at Brian, who cowered slightly in his seat at the kitchen table, empty plate in front of him, omelette in his tummy. He was seeing something that he never would have got at home. His dad didn't start screaming if there weren't enough eggs. He might be a bit cheesed off and tut and make a fuss, but he didn't go ballistic like mine. Shouting and screaming. Effing and blinding. Going mad, shouting about how it was his house and if I didn't like it I could bloody well leave. At one point I even thought he was going to hit me, and then Brian and I were scuttling upstairs, my furious father left pacing the floor of the basement.

'Bloody hell, your dad likes his eggs, don't he?' said Brian as we stood catching our breath. His eyes darted nervously and a little more colour left his face as there was a loud crash and curse from below us.

'Yeah,' I agreed. 'He's always been fond of eggs.'

Another crash and curse from down below.

'What you going to do now?'

'Dunno,' I said.

'Well, you can't stay here. There's no telling what he'll do.'

I think at that moment Brian was more scared of my dad than I was.

'I'll tell you what,' he continued. 'Why don't you come home with me?'

'All right,' I said.

And I did.

I left Waldemar for the first time. I got married, became pregnant for the first time, then we separated. And then I went back. The house wanted me back.

Fourteen

'You're pregnant, Sally.'

It was a lady who came to do the books at the surgery. I'd woken up one morning and started vomiting. I dragged myself into work, white as a ghost, and was throwing up there, too, when she came up to me. She was a lovely lady, she really was. Very well-spoken.

'What's wrong, dear?'

'I can't stop being sick,' I managed, 'and I've got this terrible ringing in my ears.'

'Ah, really? You can't stop being sick. And you've got a ringing in your ears?'

'Yes.'

She smiled knowingly, then told me.

Oh, God. I looked at her, thinking, *No. No I can't be pregnant.*

We never . . .

Or, we *hardly* ever . . .

Because my married life with Brian wasn't exactly testing the bedsprings, let's put it that way. Marry in haste, they say, repent at leisure, which is exactly what I was doing, because it had been a mistake. Brian had taken me home to his mum and dad. I'd walked out of the hallway at Waldemar and into the light – to his house. There, his parents actually spoke to Brian and me, rather than growling at us. The house was light and warm, the atmosphere loving. His mum sat me down and offered me a cup of tea. My mum phoned that night: you send my Sally home.

'She won't come home, Beryl,' said Brian's mum, 'not after what's been said and done. She's staying here for a bit. Let it settle.'

'Shall we get married?' said Brian, later.

'Yeah,' I said. We'd been making plans anyway. He just wanted to bring it forward.

So we did. We got married in July 1971. In the meantime I didn't go back to Waldemar once, not even to collect clothes; I ended up buying new ones. None of my family came to the wedding, which was at Chelsea Registry Office. I had a headache that day. And what a headache that was. After the vows had been exchanged I looked at him and said, 'What have I done?'

His face fell. 'What do you mean?'

'I shouldn't have done this,' I said. 'We shouldn't have got married.'

The headache got worse. It got so bad I couldn't go to the reception and they had to have it without me. We found a flat together, and were making plans to move into a house. Then I started getting sick in the mornings and the lady at the surgery told me that . . .

Oh God. Just hearing it was enough to make me throw up again. Shortly afterwards I was seeing a doctor and not long after that, getting a phone call from a receptionist at the surgery: 'Your test's come back positive.'

'And what does that mean?' I asked. *Duh*.

'It means you're definitely having a baby,' she said, as though addressing a child. 'You're pregnant.'

I've got to leave him, I thought. It flashed across my mind as swiftly and simply as that. I was so sorry – so desperately sorry – but I didn't love him and I should never have married him. And I knew that if I had the baby, and if Brian saw the baby and fell in love with it, then I might never be able to get away. I had to leave him.

Our flat had been sold, netting us what was a huge amount of money in 1971: £20,000. We'd bought a house in Fulham and as we were waiting to move in we were staying in a flat owned by my grandpa who, after Nanny Gladys died, had temporarily moved out of Waldemar Avenue.

There were days to go before the big move, when I turned to Brian and told him I wasn't coming. Sorry, I said to him, I can't do it. I don't love you. I'm going to leave. I want to be back at my mum and dad's.

It broke his heart. I can't pretend otherwise. In the circumstances I tried to get out as quickly and cleanly as possible, but he really didn't deserve the heartache – one of the reasons I'm not using his real name.

Anyway, he drove me back to my mum's. He'd just bought a new Jaguar and as we drove he assured me everything would be all right; told me that I probably just needed a bit of time, that I'd come round. That was what we always said back then, whenever anybody seemed to be acting strangely. They'd 'come round'. I sat staring out of the window of the Jaguar, watching the streets, shops and houses flash past, until we were on Fulham Road, then turning onto Waldemar Avenue.

I hadn't been back since the day I walked out. The day I'd left was a warm summer afternoon. Today was a crisp February day, a Saturday. Dad would be out, doing something to do with his birds. Mum would be in, probably vacuuming if I knew her.

'We're going to have a good life,' said Brian as we pulled up to the kerb. A good life? The fact that we had all that money, I suppose. He couldn't see into my heart, though.

'I can't be with you,' I told him, voice breaking, 'I'm sorry.'

I stepped out of the car and onto the pavement.

'Look,' he was saying, leaning across the passenger seat to speak to me. 'I'll pick you up at five pm.' His voice was bright, full of hope. He still thought ... oh, it's heartbreaking.

And I wasn't even listening. I was standing on the pavement staring up at number 13. It towered over me. Forcing me into its shadow.

The car drew away. I really do think he drove away believing everything would be all right.

I climbed the couple of steps to the front door and knocked. I could hear the sound of the vacuum cleaner from inside. Just hearing it and knowing it was being operated by my mum – I suddenly had this desperate need to be with her. I knocked again. Inside the vacuum cleaner switched off, its roar dying, replaced by silence. The door opened.

'Hello, mum,' I said.

She stared at me for what felt like a long time, then: 'Hello, love.'

'Oh, mum,' I said, tears coming now.

'What's the matter?' she was saying. 'Sally, what's wrong, love?'

'I can't live with him, mum. I'm going to leave Brian.'

'When?'

'Now.'

'Now?'

'Yes, this is it. This is me leaving Brian.'

'You'd better come in, love,' she said.

I walked into the hallway. I think I've already said, but it all happens in the hall at Waldemar Avenue.

And the poor man. He came back to pick me up at five pm, just as he said he would, and ended up having words with my mum on the steps; he wouldn't leave without seeing me. She was having none of it and it got heated. Ended up with her hitting him over the head with the vacuum cleaner – well, not the whole vacuum cleaner, just the nozzle bit.

He phoned continually, sent flowers every day. It was dreadful, the guilt. I mean, everything's turned out all right for him now and he has a family of his own, but I broke that man's heart.

I didn't see him again until after the baby was born, when the two of us went to the bank and I signed everything over to him: the house, all our money, everything.

I was two months pregnant when I left him. I had to

go then. It would have been worse if the baby had been born. No, it had to be then. I went back to Waldemar at the beginning of February 1972 and by the end of that month I was in hospital.

I guess it saved me, in a way, from what could have been a really horrendous situation. I was glad to be back at Waldemar, but there were still – how can I put this? – 'issues' there, mainly around my dad. Put it this way, I wasn't going to be cooking any omelettes in a hurry. Plus, nobody told Brian where I was, so at least I was spared having to face him as he bombarded my mum with phone calls and flowers. But any domestic problems swiftly became irrelevant when I found myself in hospital, suffering from hyper-tension: too much protein in the urine. The symptoms of pre-eclampsia, in other words. I'd gone to the Queen Charlotte for an ante-natal visit and the next thing I knew they were preparing a bed for me.

I remained in hospital until the birth, suffering from blurred vision, high blood pressure and constant sickness, hormones all over the place. They had me on an IV drip, plus a saline drip, and prescribed complete rest. For most of the seven months I had to lie in a darkened room at the Queen Charlotte. And it was such a hot summer as well, which didn't exactly help matters.

Almost at full term, my blood pressure climbed very, very high. My parents were called and told the hospital wanted to induce me; because the pre-eclampsia was so bad I was in danger of suffering from a stroke. But they took my blood pressure and I'd improved slightly.

'Let's leave it another day,' said the doctor.

They did. And the next day, my daughter Jemma was born.

I won't go into the gory details, but it was a 32-hour labour, and they gave me an epidural which left me paralysed for five days. It had just been introduced then; I suppose they hadn't perfected the procedure, but it left me without the use of my arms and legs for a while. All I could move was my head. Jemma was whisked off because she was so tiny; she'd end up staying in hospital for a month. Meanwhile, the hospital thought they'd left something inside me, so I was subjected to almost daily scans to find a clip that had mysteriously disappeared.

They were terrified, first because of the paralysis, then because of the clip. I remember one day, lying flat on my back, in agony, being taken for an X-ray. And it never showed up, not from that day to this. In the end they were shrugging and saying it must have been swept away.

The upshot of all this medical misery was that I was told I shouldn't have any more children for at least two years, and if and when I did, not to have an epidural. I took both bits of advice.

'Ain't dad going to come and see her?' I said one afternoon, sitting in the hospital bed with Jemma in my arms, staring down in love and wonder at this little marvel I had produced. While I had the paralysis, I hadn't been able to focus all of my love on her; she'd been taken away anyway. So when I saw her now, I held on to her, cupping her tiny head in my hand, inspecting hands and fingers that clawed and gripped at me. Those days, I felt so much love blooming inside me I thought I would burst. You'll know that feeling if you've got a kid yourself. You'll know how it takes you by surprise and knocks you for six. You think you know what love is, and then you have a child, and then you *really* know what love is. You never want to let that go once you've had it.

That night, dad came, and for the first time – a week after I'd given birth – I had both parents in the room to see Jemma. And something happened.

They were only 37 when I had her, you see. It's nothing, is it? No age. Plenty of people are having their first children in their mid-30s; they're ready for it then. This was my mum and dad's grandchild.

Perhaps they weren't ready for children when they had us. Maybe they were ready now, at 37.

That night at the hospital, I watched dad hold Jemma and he changed before my eyes. He softened. He became a different man. They both changed.

Fifteen

I met John on New Year's Eve, 1973. These days he's everything to me, he's the reason the sun rises. Back then he was a lifeline, a way out, an escape from Waldemar Avenue and the spirits there.

It was one of my mum and dad's parties. Oh, those parties. My mum absolutely loved throwing them. The basement would be packed with people. We pushed all the furniture up against the walls to make a space in the middle for dancing. Dad would be in the kitchen, doing his bit, serving drinks and letting mum get on with the business of being the hostess – and she didn't need much encouraging to do that. The music would be up loud, so conversation was conducted by shouting, nodding and smiling. The air was thick with perfume and cigarette smoke, which hung in the air in layers. People would sit on the stairs going up from the basement and you'd have to pick your way past them to get up and down, smiling at the guests who were sitting there, chatting and smoking.

'Hello, Sal.'

'You all right there, love? Am I in your way?'

Then into the basement where the smoke would seem to part like curtains before you. The music was louder; there was dancing in the middle of the room and mum, always mum, holding court, glass of wine in one hand, cigarette in the other, looking like Liz Taylor.

There was a buzz about this particular party. Well, it was New Year's Eve, wasn't it, and that's always a bit special. But it felt like an important one. The whole family was together. Mum was a grandmother. Not even out of her 30s and she was a granny. But she was determined not to act like one. Oh no, not my mum.

I was kind of seeing this bloke at the time. He was more of a friend, really. He'd been at a club in Fulham that night and told some friends he was going to a party along Waldemar Avenue, and asked did they want to come.

'Yeah, sure,' they said.

Except one of them, who said, 'Nah, I don't think I'll bother.'

'Oh come on, John,' they cajoled him.

'Nah,' he said.

'Oh, come on.'

(Things could have been so different. I shudder to think. I absolutely shudder to think that I might never have met my John.)

'Oh all right, then.'

And they set off on their way to Waldemar. They followed the sound of the music to number 13 where somebody let them in and they walked into the hall, to the door that led down into the basement, stepping over guests sitting at the top of the stairs, picking their way down into the furnace. The perfume and cigarette smoke. Music and laughter. Cheese and pineapple on cocktail sticks. Sausage rolls.

And me. I was there, too. I was standing chatting to some of mum's friends who were asking me about the baby. Jemma was then 16 months old, upstairs in bed asleep.

'We heard you had a baby. Beryl was saying . . .'

I glanced across at my mother, the 30-something granny. She adored Jemma. Doted on her. So did dad. The pair of them with Jemma, well, it was like seeing two different people. My dad was all over Jemma; he couldn't get enough of her. He'd look at her, rapt. I'd never seen him so affectionate. Not over anything that didn't have wings and feathers, anyway.

And then I saw them coming down the stairs. First my friend – he thought he was my boyfriend, but he wasn't really, he was just a friend. Nothing had happened, if you know what I mean. And behind him came another man. He wore a black polo neck, a herringbone jacket over it, black shoes and trousers. He stood at the bottom of the stairs, taking in our party. Then he made his way over to some seats at the side of the room.

'Who's that fella?' I asked my friend.

'Him? That's Buster.'

'Who's he, then?'

'He's a greengrocer. He runs the football team. Why?'

I was looking at him. He was oblivious to me, of course, talking to one of the blokes he'd arrived with. But I was getting this feeling, strong as you like: *You've got to talk to him.*

Got to.

'Hello,' I said. I had to shout.

'Hello.'

'I'm Sally. They say you're Buster.'

And I sat down. Never been backward in coming forward, me.

'Actually,' he said, as I settled beside him, 'I'd rather you didn't call me Buster. My name's John. I'm trying to get this lot to call me John.'

(And you know what he told me later? That it was the first time he'd ever said that to anyone. It was only at that moment that something he'd been thinking about became a fully formed decision. I sat down next to him and he stopped being Buster. He became John. Not that he knew it then, of course, but he became *my* John.)

We chatted. Next thing, Jemma had woken up. I guess one of the guests lounging in the hall must have heard her, called down and my mum answered the call before I had a chance to. She'd collected Jemma and brought her back down to the basement, where she began fussing over her. Guests gathered around. Jemma was walking by then but she sat, sleepy, in the middle of the floor, looking quizzically as beaming guests jostled to see her, my mum looking on.

On a chair at the side of the room, I watched, seeing the scene through John's eyes: a doting mum showing off her daughter. For a split-second it occurred to me to let him believe exactly that, but something inside me said, *No, you've got to tell him.* Of course I should tell him. Why not?

'She's mine,' I said, finding myself fill with pride as I said it, then adding, hurriedly, 'I'm not with the father anymore.'

'Oh,' he said, 'right.' Not bothered at all, of course. If he'd been bothered he wouldn't have been the man I thought he was.

And I watched my mum doting over Jemma some more. Looking across the room I saw my dad gazing on, and felt a sharp dart of hurt at the look on his face. Oh my goodness, over the last 16 months I'd seen him sit Jemma on his knee countless times. He'd bought a silver teething ring; almost every day he arrived home from work with a new present for Jemma. I watched it happening. Was I jealous? Resentful? I don't know. I'm not sure if I understood my emotions then and I still don't. All I know is I was seeing my father lavish so much love on that baby. The person Jemma would grow up to know wouldn't be the dad I recognized. This was a different person.

He'd take her out to see the pigeons. Growing up, one of the things my parents constantly argued about was the fact that Gina and I weren't allowed in the back garden.

'Why can't my girls go out there?' my mum would demand.

But his answer was final. Nobody went out to the coops but him.

Him and Jemma now, of course. During the summer he'd been taking her out to the decking and sitting her down. I'd watch them from the scullery window.

The other thing that summer just gone had been the holiday. We were supposed to go to the Isle of Wight. Dad never came, of course, he couldn't bear to be away from his birds for any length of time, so it was just the girls, and for some reason – I don't recall quite how it happened – there wasn't room for everybody on the trip. Mum offered to take Jemma and like a fool, I let her. What was better, for her to go without me, or for neither of us to go? I thought I knew at the time. I thought it would be selfish to make her stay at home. I'm not so sure now. All I know is, it broke me, thinking of Jemma away without me.

About halfway through the holiday, mum rang and I got tearful on the phone, telling her I missed Jemma.

'I'm not having this,' she snapped, as though I had no right to ask. 'I'm not having this. Put yer father on the phone this minute.'

Like I had no right to ask. I'm her mum, I wanted to scream. Shake some bloody sense into them. *I'm her mum.*

That summer's night, with my dad glaring at me, like, *What have you done to upset your mother now*, I made up my mind: I had to get out. Not long after I announced I was going to get a council flat. I even had someone from the council come round to inspect my accommodation. See if I was a deserving-enough case. I wasn't, of course. The house was practically a mansion.

'You'll never get a council flat,' said the woman on the doorstep, leaving me to close the door and sigh loudly in the hallway, the house seeming to mock me. Don't think you're getting away that easily.

Only now here was this man, this John. You might think that with all that was going on at Waldemar I'd have shacked up with the first bloke to so much as raise an eyebrow at me. Well you'd be wrong. The sort-of boyfriend wanted me to marry him but I wasn't about to make that mistake again. Of course I wanted to leave Waldemar (I *needed* to leave Waldemar) but I'd already made the mistake of settling for second best and didn't plan on doing it again.

Later, at the doorway, when the party was over I said, 'Well, when am I going to see you again?' and he looked a bit taken aback. Me being so forward, plus the fact that I was sort-of seeing his friend. 'Not sure,' he said, 'down the pub?'

And that was it, I watched him go.

Valentine's Day came around and I still hadn't seen him again. I bought him a card ('You promised me we'd go for a drink,' I wrote in it, even though he'd done nothing of the sort) and sent it to the greengrocer's shop. Of course it turned out I'd sent it to the wrong shop, but it found its way to him, and one night when I was at work – still working as a dental nurse – the phone rang.

'Hello, is that Sally?' said the voice at the other end of the line.

'Yes,' I said.

'It's John,' he said, and my heart almost burst its way out my ribcage. 'I've got your card.'

'You have? Oh, you have. That's great.'

'I'd really like to see you.'

'Oh,' I said, hardly able to believe it. 'Well that would be lovely.'

And then he said, 'Oh, sorry, love, it's not really John.'

My heart sank. I suddenly felt like the world's biggest loser.

'Well . . . who are you, then?' I managed, cheeks burning with the shame of it, thinking, Oh God and I sounded so enthusiastic. I must have sounded like the world's biggest fool.

'It's Derek,' he said.

And with my mind racing, not really in control of my thoughts, I blurted, 'What, my Uncle Derek?'

Oh, you silly mare. What was I saying?

'No, it's Derek who works with John.'

Who? What?

'Look, I'm sorry, love, I'll go and get him.'

It was all I could do not to slam the phone down there and then. And then must have felt guilty about his joke, Derek, because I discovered later that he told John I was lovely and that John should speak to me right now and that he should definitely ask me out for a drink.

So he did. And once certain things had been sorted out (this sort-of boyfriend being the main one), we were a courting couple. And after something else had been sorted out (in other words, my divorce) we were able to get married. I could at last leave Waldemar. I'd been saved, or so I thought.

We'd been together two years. Apparently his dad had said just one sentence when John told him he'd started seeing a married woman who had a child: 'You're asking for trouble there, son.' Well, he wasn't wrong about that. But we'd been together long enough now for them to get used to the idea. My mum and dad? Well, that was a separate issue. They were keen for us to live together but they wanted us at Waldemar. With us there they could continue to lavish lots of love on Jemma.

'Tomorrow, I'm telling my mum that we're going to live together,' I told John, as we stepped out into the night.

'No, don't,' he said.

'Oh . . .' Well that stopped me in my tracks. I'd thought he felt the same way about me as I did about him. Hopelessly, desperately in love. 'Why not?' I asked, trying not to sound too wounded.

'Because we should get married.'

'Oh,' I said.

One divorce later and we were married. It was the best day of my life. February 15, 1975, at Fulham Registry Office, followed by a blessing at St Peter's Church (I was a divorced woman, you see, I couldn't get married in a church) and then a reception at the Labour Rooms on Fulham Road.

For six months we both lived together at Waldemar as we made our new house in Orbain Road habitable. With John there, I started to see my life with an outsider's eyes. I saw my controlling mother, my simmering father. One evening, my mother and Gina were arguing over who should change Jemma's nappy.

'Hang on a minute,' said John. 'She's Sally's daughter. Sally should change her nappy,' and with that my father left the room, slamming the door so violently behind him that the glass cracked.

And, finally, I left Waldemar. It wasn't an easy parting, there were words and bad feelings. There were no cards or tear-stained farewells or good wishes. Instead, John, Jemma and I moved to Orbain Road, a house that we'd virtually rebuilt so it was almost like brand new. And there a new life awaited us. John loved Jemma as his own. He adopted her, and I remember very clearly being told that we should tell Jemma about her true parentage as soon as was practical. Don't wait, we were advised, but, well, we chose to ignore that bit of advice; we'd tell her when she reached eighteen we decided. Looking back, God, that was a big mistake.

Anyway, in the meantime we were just like any other family. And me? I felt like I'd been saved. Saved from an unhappy marriage. I wouldn't have to worry about my surname anymore either: whether it was West or Thatcher. I was Mrs Morgan now. I was Sally Morgan.

Sixteen

Our house on Orbain Road was a tiny terrace. We'd bought it from John's mum and dad, with plans to do it up, and we did most of the work before moving in. We'd put in a bathroom, a brand new staircase and installed a new kitchen among other things, although there were still finishing touches needed when we moved in. John was still working at the greengrocer's then. Still with Derek the practical joker. So he'd be getting up and going to work at four am. He was doing most of the buying at that time, so he was needed at the market. Not exactly up with the lark – even larks don't get up that early, but that was the job. He'd get up, kiss me goodbye and leave the house. It was summer by then, the mornings very light, and I had old curtains up that weren't the best, so the sunshine would often keep me awake. I remember one morning, when we'd been in the new house a week or so, I was lying in bed, shortly after he'd left, and I heard the front door swing open.

In bed, I sighed, thinking, 'Silly bugger's left the bloody door open.' Now I was going to have to get up and close it. Damn.

But I wasn't worried. It wasn't as though somebody was going to come in off the street. It wasn't that sort of area. Not that sort of street. We'd only been there a matter of days but already we knew virtually everyone along the road, plus of course John's parents had lived in the house, so no, not scared. Just lying there with a sinking heart, the way you feel when you've got to get out of your nice, warm bed and go downstairs to close the door because your big doughnut of a husband has left the front door open, bless his heart. Then I heard it. Pitter-patter on the floor. The unmistakeable sound of a dog's paws on the floor.

Back then, dogs used to run around the streets. People would go to work and let the dog out. So naturally I assumed that one had found its way inside, and thinking, Oh bloody hell, a dog's got in, I sat up, just about to get out of bed and sort it out when the bedroom door opened and in walked a dog. A black and white dog. I stared at it. I wasn't frightened; growing up in Waldemar I was more than used to dogs. But there was something about this one that made me freeze. As it walked across the room it turned its head to look at me, regarding me calmly as though it owned the place, walking towards the bedroom wall. For a split-second I thought the daft dog was going to walk slap-bang into the wall. But it didn't. It walked straight through.

I smiled and dropped back onto the bed. I'd left the spirits at Waldemar Road, but it looked as though I'd found at least one new one, and later that night I told John about it. Of course, he was getting used to all this sort of stuff.

'What did it look like?' he asked me.

'Oh, John, I'll never forget,' I said. 'It had a black body

and a white face, with maybe a few spots of black on it, like . . .'

'That was Blackie,' interrupted John, jolted by a sudden memory.

'You what?'

'That was Blackie. Years ago we had a dog called Blackie. Years ago, he . . . which wall did he walk into?'

I indicated the bedroom wall. John looked at it, then downwards, trying to figure something out. 'Blackie ran out into the road,' he said. 'He ran out of the front door. Directly below this spot.'

He looked at me. 'I've never mentioned that dog to you,' he said. 'How did you . . . ?' Tailing off, looking from me to the spot in the wall where the spirit of his boyhood dog had disappeared.

'I told you,' I said. 'I told you that I could see things.'

'You told me that you *know* things,' he corrected, and he was no doubt thinking of the time shortly after we'd got together that I confidently informed him that we were going to get married and stay together for the rest of our lives. That time he'd given me a sideways look and said, 'You what? How on earth do you know that?' Lucky it was the real thing, eh? Otherwise he'd have run a mile.

'Oh,' I'd said then. 'I know things.'

And I suppose he'd put it down to me being pushy, or some kind of women's intuition; and not given it too much thought.

And now I said, 'Well, I see things, too.'

'You "know" things and you "see" things?'

'Yes.'

How do you explain? I couldn't. Back then I was still trying to make sense of it myself. I hadn't yet started calling myself a medium or a psychic.

'Tell me again,' he said, regarding me with fresh eyes. 'Tell me what you saw.'

I made a believer out of John.

A short while later, we were in bed one night when I heard a noise. *Click, click.* It was the middle of the night, God knows what time, and John was fast asleep beside me. *Click, click.* My dad had had the wardrobe made for us and it was the type that shut with a ball and clasp. That kind of wardrobe closed with a very distinctive click: the same sound I could hear now.

Click, click.

Funny, I couldn't remember leaving a window open. I sat up, looking over at the window and half-expecting to see the curtain billowing in a breeze. It hung straight, so, tutting, I got out to check, padding across the bedroom floor and pulling the curtain back to fasten the window.

Click, click.

It was shut. The window was shut. Oh, but there was another window. I checked that. Also closed.

Click, click.

I went to the wardrobe and checked the door. It was closed as usual. Opening and closing it made the same noise that I was hearing yet it seemed securely fastened when it was closed. Ah, I thought, maybe this house has got a few more tricks up its sleeves. I was grinning to myself as I got back in bed, thinking maybe I should wake up John and tell him Blackie was back.

I lay back down and closed my eyes ready to sleep.

Then I felt something by my feet, exactly as though someone had sat on the edge of the bed. Slowly, I opened my eyes and looked down the bed. There, perched on the end of it, was a man.

He was sitting on my feet. Can you believe that? I had a spirit sitting on my feet. *Bloody cheek*. For a moment or so I studied him: he was in silhouette, just sitting there, looking for all the world like he owned the place.

And you know what I did then? This is how comfortable I felt: I pulled the sheets up over my head and went back to sleep. The next day, even just walking round the house, I could still somehow feel him on my feet. Weird, that. Almost like an impression of him that was taking a long time to go.

I told John about him, but he had no idea who he might be and in the end we decided he must an old, old spirit wanting to see what we'd done to the house. The *click, click* of the cupboard I'd heard that night? It was the spirit admiring my dad's handiwork, I'm sure of it.

He came again. A couple of times. He never actually trapped my feet again (let's face it, it can't have been all that comfy for him) but he definitely sat on my bed on other occasions, and each time I'd wake John and tell him about it, relieved I finally had someone with whom I could share all this stuff. He didn't mind that his wife had had strange men sitting on the end of her bed (well, he might have minded if they'd been alive, obviously) and he didn't insist I was mistaken, or seeing things, or any of the dismissals I'd grown up hearing from my mother. With mum, I had to go through such a rigmarole. I used to have to tell her about my 'funny dreams', even if I hadn't been asleep. So if I'd seen a spirit, or knew something about somebody, I had to dress it up for her, even though I strongly believed she knew exactly what was going on. She should have done because she'd had exactly the same thing with Nanny Gladys, but even so, we had to go through this little dance each time.

You can't really blame her. It's asking a lot of someone to accept that their daughter is seeing spirits, communicating with the other side. For me, it just increased the confusion, though. Why was I seeing these things? What brought them on? Mum used to try and explain it away by telling me I only saw stuff when I was ill. She did that because, to be fair, the visions and knowings often *did* increase when I was under the weather – why that was I'm not entirely sure. Perhaps it was something to do with being more vulnerable and therefore more open; perhaps spirits seeing me suffering and wanting to help. I don't know, I really don't. But even if I've forgotten many of the things I saw back then – and certainly I very rarely remember those times when I just 'came out' with something – I know full well they didn't just happen when I was ill; they happened all of the time. I didn't know how to stop them, I didn't know how to control them (and oh, the times I yearned for Nanny Gladys to explain my gift to me), but I knew there was a bit more to it than me being poorly.

As I say, I can't blame my mum, really. There would be other things I'd blame her for, later in life, things I will never, ever forgive her for. But I don't blame her for that.

One thing I knew: I should have been scared, but I wasn't. I wasn't seeing a ghost, not in the horror movie sense of the word. He was someone on another plane who had as much right to be there as I did. I never used to try and communicate with the spirits I saw. Sometimes a spirit will try and make contact, like Granny Brodie, but most of the time they were simply part of the fabric of the house; doing whatever it is they did. How can I explain? It's a bit like when you're sitting watching TV with a mug of hot tea and a biscuit, and the cat comes to curl up at your feet. For me, it was like that with spirits. They were there. They were often around. But we didn't really share the same reality.

Does that make sense? Most people didn't see them, of course. I'm one of the few. But I think what I realized as I was lying there, my feet trapped by the silent guy sitting at the bottom of the bed, was that I was becoming so accustomed to this stuff, so used to it. Somehow I was sharing my life with spirits, with these knowings that seemed to freak out other people, but the older I got, the more turbulence I had in my own life, the more I was beginning to feel at ease with them; the more I was coming to see them as friends.

These days I often get asked about getting rid of spirits and I always refuse. I tell people the spirits have as much right to be there as they do. Which is absolutely true. If your house has a spirit and you can see it, the last thing you should be thinking about is getting rid of it. Congratulations, it's proof that you've got a touch of psychic ability. You should be pleased.

There's an exception that proves every rule, though, which is why we needed an exorcism at our next house.

Seventeen

The first time I saw the spirit at Beverley Way I was outside in the back garden. We'd moved to New Malden from Orbain Road in search of more space for our expanding family. By this time I had a second daughter, Rebecca, and once again, I'd spent much of my pregnancy in hospital with pre-eclampsia but, as with Jemma, it was a small price to pay. I now had two adorable little girls and a fantastic husband and I look back on those days with such affection. I'd given up work and I really felt I was bonding with my two girls. Such great days.

Plus, there was this new house. Beverley Way in New Malden. We got it for next to nothing but that's because it was in such a state. I remember the day we moved in. Rebecca, then about 18 months old, went running into the garden and we lost her the grass was that high. Waist high, it was, like a wheat field, and little Rebecca just completely disappeared. We spent many frantic moments trying to find her.

Originally, it had been owned by a couple called Mr and Mrs Walters, according to our new neighbours, Alma and Albert. But Mrs Walters had died, and the house had been bought by a family who had let it go a little. I don't think Mrs Walters was very happy about that. Poor, tormented soul.

It was her I saw in the back garden. One beautiful summer's day, I was out there with the girls, and I think I'd been chatting to Alma over the garden fence. It was exactly like something out of a 1970s sitcom, chatting to your neighbour over the garden fence. Anyway, we were out there enjoying the sun when something caught my eye – something in the house. A movement. I stopped what I was doing. Weeding, perhaps. Or playing with the girls. Whatever it was, I stopped, straightened and stared back at the house, shielding my eyes.

And there it was again. A movement at the window of one of the back bedrooms. It was a woman. There was a woman standing at one of the windows.

'Oh,' I said. Just like that. Except I must've had said it sharply and loudly enough for Alma to stop what she was doing on her side and come to the garden fence.

'Are you all right, Sally?' she asked.

I remember, it was so quiet. The only noise was the two girls playing.

'Um . . .' I said, still staring at the window. Which was empty. The woman had gone.

'Sally, what's up?' pressed Alma.

'I could've sworn I saw a woman at our window,' I said, pointing. 'I'm sure of it. I'm sure there was someone standing there.' And you know what I was thinking? I'd left the front door open. I'd left the bloody front door open and a mad woman had walked into our house.

'Oh, that'll be Mrs Walters,' said Alma, matter-of-factly.

I swung to look at her. 'You what?'

'Mrs Walters. You know. Who used to live here.'

She was still here. I looked up to the window where I'd seen her. Standing in the garden I hadn't seen her face properly, she was more of a shape, but even so there had been a sadness about her, like an aura that seemed to surround her. Either that, or I just somehow knew. Mrs Walters was an unhappy spirit. I wondered if I'd ever see her again.

I did, not long later. It was another one of those mornings when John had left the house at some ungodly hour and I was snoozing in bed. I'd been lying there half-awake when I felt the sheets move. They moved around my chest and I realized I was being tucked into bed. Me, half-asleep, thinking, It's John. He's come back into the house for some reason and he's tucking me in. How sweet of him. And as I was thinking that, the sheets were smoothed down, then I felt a hand pat them, the way you do when you're making a bed and want it to look nice and smart. Then, a single thought pierced my sleep-fogged brain.

That's not John.

I sat up in bed. Just in time to see the figure of Mrs Walters – the same woman I'd seen at the window – moving around my bedroom, then leaving through the door, which was closed.

She'd tucked me in. How weird is that, I thought. Mrs Walters has just tucked me in. I had a duvet then. Duvets were just becoming popular in the UK; sheets were soon to be obsolete. And it was folded over. I suppose because Mrs Walters had no experience with duvets, she tried to fold it as you would a sheet, but she'd ended up folding it over my waist where it was now, very neat and precise.

Later that day, with the back door open and my two girls playing out in the garden – how they loved that garden – I saw Alma over the garden fence.

'Alma,' I said, checking neither Jemma nor Rebecca would be able to hear us.

'Yes, love?'

'Could I have a word?'

She approached the fence. Funny, I don't think she ever came into my house, or me into hers. It was a relationship conducted almost entirely over a garden fence.

'I think I saw Mrs Walters again this morning.'

'Ah,' she said, not shocked, 'where was she this time?'

'In the bedroom.'

'Ah . . .'

'Alma, what did she do? What was her occupation?'

'Mrs Walters? She was a midwife, love. Why?'

I nodded, feeling a tingle. A feeling suspended halfway between a thrill and a sudden realization that Mrs Walters *knew*. She'd been tucking me in, taking care of me. All because she knew that . . .

'I'm pregnant,' I told Alma.

Perhaps that was why Mrs Walters left me alone: her midwifery instincts at work. But she was an unhappy spirit, and she made her presence felt, even to the rest of my family. She began turning lights on and off. She would open and close windows and doors. At first I didn't tell the rest of the family about her and I'd try to explain away the noises the way you do; the way people who don't believe in spirits will try to do. So I'd hear myself coming out with all these things, like, 'Oh, it must be the electrics,' just like my dad used to do, looking at me from his chair, curious. 'You must have closed the window and forgotten you did it.' Or, 'It must have been the wind, love.'

Privately, I knew it was Mrs Walters. And she was opening windows and doors because she was unhappy; she wanted to leave.

'How did she die?' I asked Alma over the garden fence another day.

'I've no idea, love, sorry. I think she died in the house, though. You could try asking their son. He used to live round here.'

I went knocking on doors but couldn't find anybody related to the Walters. Dead end.

Meanwhile, the problems with the doors and windows stepped up. Mrs Walters knew I could see her. You know those films where someone's stranded on a desert island; they see a ship in the distance and they start frantically signalling? For her it was like that. I was the ship and she was desperately trying to catch my attention.

'I'm trying to help you, darling,' I told her in a quiet moment when I sensed her around me. 'I'm doing me best.'

The poor thing, though. She was impatient. She sensed that I would be going to hospital soon, suffering from my usual pregnant bout of pre-eclampsia. She knew I'd be going away and became more and more anxious.

'We've got a ghost in here,' said John one day. That

morning he'd stood and watched a window opening and closing by itself. 'It ain't the wind is it, Sally? We've got a spirit in here.'

'It's Mrs Walters,' I admitted and told him about her.

Shortly after, Jemma piped up one morning: 'There was a woman in my bedroom last night,' and John's eyes met mine over the table. We couldn't really have that. We couldn't have Mrs Walters scaring the children.

'You really do want to go, don't you?' I said to her, when we were alone. But there was no reply.

Every day I took the kids to school. After that there was usually some shopping to do, bits and pieces, a loaf of bread, some milk. I'd take the cutting into New Malden, which brought me out onto Christchurch Road, where there was a church. Walking past most days, I'd say hello to the gardeners, but this particular day I stopped, asking one of them, 'Is the verger around?'

The gardener took the opportunity to stop and lean on his garden fork. 'He is. You want a word?'

Yes, I did.

Inside the church, I told the verger my story. 'Look,' I began, 'this is going to sound crazy to you, but . . .'

He listened carefully, nodding gravely. He looked at my baby bump and told me he'd let the vicar know I'd been in. Next thing I knew, I'd spoken to the vicar, and he was recommending we had an exorcism.

In the meantime, I'd had my third child. Another little girl, this one we called Fern. And I suppose that was what finally decided me. We now had three little girls in that house at Beverley Way and we couldn't share it with a disgruntled spirit, even if it was old Mrs Walters. We'd have to have the exorcism.

The girls went to a neighbour and we were visited by the vicar accompanied by a bishop, who was the exorcist.

'Do you want a cuppa?' I said, and for a while all four of us sat chatting, drinking our tea. It was a nice day, sun streaming through the windows and making shapes on the carpet. John and I were in our summer gear, and even the two churchmen were casually dressed, just dog collars to identify their vocation. The whole scene, it was nothing like you'd expect. I suppose we both half expected them to arrive at midnight, smack-bang in the middle of a thunderstorm, and start chanting or something, like a scene from *The Exorcist*. Instead, it was so . . . normal. More like afternoon tea with the Waltons than a Hammer Horror.

'All my life I've seen things,' I told the bishop. I don't know why I told him. In the hope he'd have answers for me, I suppose.

He nodded. 'And you feel spirits in this house?'

'Just Mrs Walters.'

At the mention of her name the air seemed to move around us, a tiny, silken disturbance. John and the vicar sat oblivious to it; only the exorcist and I seemed to notice. He tilted his head upwards slightly, as though sniffing something in the air.

'I can sense something here,' he told me. 'There's a presence here. Shall we begin?'

He told us we would have to kneel in each room.

'Kneel in each room?' said John, shooting me a look that said, *You're having a bloody laugh.*

129

'That's right,' confirmed the exorcist. We had to do that while he read out an incantation and sprinkled holy water (and all of a sudden it was starting to feel like a proper exorcism), and we began, right there in the front room. John and I knelt on the carpet as the exorcist called for the spirit to leave in peace then shook a bottle of holy water, dispensing drops of it into the room. We did it in each room and when it was over we said goodbye to the exorcist and the vicar and closed the door behind them.

We stood in the hallway, expecting what, I'm not sure.

'Is she still here, then?' said John. Bless him. He expected me to know. As if I was equipped with a pair of Bionic Ghost-Finding Eyes.

'I don't know, love,' I told him, 'I really don't.'

Or did I? There was something different about the house. Definitely. I could feel it. As we went back to the kitchen for a post-exorcism cup of tea I said a silent farewell to Mrs Walters, hoping that I'd got it right; that she really did want to leave. She was restless, I knew that much. Either way, as she had been a midwife I knew she would have respected my decision. You've got to protect your kids, haven't you?

Eighteen

I was shopping on New Malden High Street one day when I felt a tap on my shoulder, turned round and saw a woman standing there, heavily pregnant.

I didn't know it, but things were about to change for me. I'd never be the same again.

I had the pram with me, Fern inside, a tiny baby. It was one of those proper old prams, a coach-built pram, and it had a toddler seat attached, where Rebecca could sit. Jemma was at school by then.

'Excuse me,' she said, 'but are you Sally?' She had a pram too, I noticed, a baby inside. A right pair of New Malden housewives we must have looked, standing there in the high street, three-and-a-half kids between us. Shoppers trudged past weighed down with bags; cars and buses made their way along the road.

'Yes, I'm Sally,' I said, my mind racing the way it does in situations like that. She knew me but I just couldn't place her. Was it from school? Work?

'It's me,' she said.

I was smiling, pulling the face. The 'I'm really sorry, but I don't think I remember you' face.

'Oh, you know,' she prompted, smiling.

But I still couldn't place her, saying, 'I'm really sorry,

love, I've got a mind like a sieve, me. I just can't remember you.'

She didn't seem too bothered; was still smiling at me. 'Tell you what,' she said, 'do you remember going dancing at the White Lion in Putney?'

Well, yes, I did. Aged 14 or 15, I'd gone there a lot. What nights out we used to have. Didn't help much, though. I still didn't remember her.

'You haven't changed a bit,' she said. And actually she was right. I was tiny in those days; I'd hardly changed since my teens.

'You must have . . .' I tried.

'Well, I wasn't pregnant then,' she laughed. 'I know – do you remember the twins?'

Ah. It was like my mind had a set of thick, red curtains obscuring all memory and suddenly they drew back.

'Oh!' I said, 'Jane and Clare. You mean Jane and Clare?'

'That's right. Jane and Clare. The twins.'

Of course, of course, I was thinking. They were twins but not identical, and we used to knock around together, going out mainly, dancing, the usual sort of stuff you do when you're 15.

'They're my cousins,' she explained. 'I'm Paula.'

Well, she was a good four or five years younger than her two cousins, which might be why I didn't instantly recognize her. She knew me, though. I must have made quite an impression, because the next thing she said, touching my arm as she did so, was, 'Here, do you still do that funny thing?'

'What funny thing?'

'You know, where you see things around people?'

'Oh, that,' I said, 'I did that around you, did I?'

'Not half,' she said, grinning. 'Don't you remember?'

'I'm not doing very well this morning, am I?' I laughed. But as I've said, I rarely ever remembered doing what Paula called 'the funny thing'.

'We were at the White Lion one night and you were dancing with this coloured guy, Bill,' said Paula.

God, yes, I thought. Bill. He was a lovely guy, Bill, but he wasn't boyfriend material. Why? My dad, of course. He wasn't the most liberal bloke in case you hadn't already worked it out.

Anyway, Paula continued, I was dancing with Bill and I told him he was going to go out with a girl called Fiona, which was news to Bill who hadn't even given Fiona a second look.

'Did I?' I said.

'Yeah,' said Paula, excited, 'you told him he'd be seeing Fiona. Bill said that you "knew". He didn't think all that much of it at the time . . .'

'How weird,' I said.

Sometimes, it's like I'm hearing about somebody else doing these things. It's difficult to explain. I take myself by surprise.

'And now guess what?'

'What?'

'They're married. Got two children.'

Something happened to me at that moment. I opened. As though something inside me switched on, doors clanged open, images and thoughts suddenly jostling for attention.

Only, I didn't want images and thoughts in my head. I told them to go. And they did.

Chonk. Like angrily switching off a telly that refuses to tune. All of a sudden my head was clear.

'Tell you what,' Paula was saying, dragging me back to the here and now, 'do you fancy a coffee?'

I was still reeling but nodded my head and we made for a nearby Wimpy, getting settled, with Paula fetching the coffees while I stayed at the table to look after the kids. And trying to get my head together.

Somehow, something Paula said had switched me on; had activated something inside me. It was talking about it. That was it. By talking about 'that funny thing you used to do' she had somehow opened me up.

And then . . .

Then I had closed it off.

The noise and hubbub of the Wimpy swirled around me. Food was served. People slurped tea and coffee from china cups, kids grizzled and played. In the middle of it all I sat oblivious to the noise around me, almost in a state of shock, mind and body alive with the sensation of a sudden understanding.

Imagine struggling to programme a video recorder for 26 years and someone finally giving you the instruction manual. Imagine trying to read a foreign language and it suddenly making sense, the words coming to life right before your eyes. That was how it felt.

She was coming back with the coffee. Paula. Slowly

and deliberately making her way down the aisle, balancing a tray with coffees for me and her, a soft drink for Rebecca, placing it on the table and sitting, saying, 'You'll never guess who I married.'

Still open. I understood it now. I could open and close. And I was still open, receiving, whatever you want to call it. Because an image of the man she married flashed into my head only he wasn't a man, he was a boy. A boy I used to sit next to at school. His name was . . .

'Richard,' I said.

'Yeah,' she said, 'that's right. You . . .'

'. . . used to sit next to him at school.'

She started as though pinched, staring across the table at me as a huge grin spread slowly across her face. 'You know, don't you?' she said. 'Who told you, then?' She was looking around the Wimpy as if she was expecting to see John sending me morse code from behind the counter.

'I just knew,' I told her, taken aback myself.

'Ooh, you. You're doing that thing again, aren't you?'

'Yes,' I said, nodding, suddenly feeling so, so weary. I've had enough now, I wanted to tell whatever force it is who sends me these messages.

The noise of the Wimpy seemed to increase. All of a sudden I felt as though I could hear every single knife scrape, every whisper, cough and chuckle. At a table across the aisle someone threw their head back and laughed and for a second or so the sound was deafening.

'I've got a picture here,' Paula was saying, digging in her bag, handing me a photograph that I took, my other hand at my temple where a headache was beginning to form. The photograph wasn't the boy at school. This was a man. A man with a moustache. My mind struggled to pair the two images.

At the other side of the restaurant a baby began to cry. The door opened and someone called, 'Hello,' manoeuvring a pram into the restaurant, a blast of traffic noise from New Malden High Street. There was a shout from the kitchen.

'This isn't . . .' I indicated the picture. Paula leaned forward, smiling. I squeezed my eyes tight shut and concentrated on forming the words. 'It's not . . . I mean, he's changed.'

'What . . . well, of course he's changed. He didn't have a bleedin' moustache at school, did he?'

'No,' I tried to laugh, passing a hand across my forehead and handing back the picture. 'Sorry, I got a bit confused.'

The noise. It was inside my head. Outside. I felt like I might have to go. Give Paula my apologies. Tell her I felt ill or something.

'We're going through a bit of a bad patch at the moment,' she was saying as I desperately tried to pull myself together. 'Richard's been made redundant from Rolls Royce.'

'Oh, love, I'm sorry to hear about that,' I said. And I was. My headache seemed to recede, as did the noise of the restaurant. For almost the first time since we sat down I was able to properly focus on Paula, and in my head I saw Richard again. The young Richard. The Richard I'd sat next to in class. Just as he was before, except this time I saw money floating down around his head. Imagine trying to picture a family member in your head. Richard was like that, but with 10-, 20-, 50-pound notes falling like snowflakes around him.

Now, in the years since then I've learnt not to interpret what I see. You come and see me and I'm not going to tell you what something means, I'll just tell you what I've seen. The meaning, that's for you to work out.

But come on. Richard had notes floating around his face.

'He's been working on a couple of cars from home, just out in the street to try and make ends meet,' Paula was saying.

'Oh, you're going to be all right, love,' I said.

She stopped, cup of coffee suspended between mouth and table. 'You what?'

'You're going to be all right. You and Richard. I can see it. You'll have so much money you won't know what to do with it all.'

'You're doing it again, aren't you?' She looked puzzled, taken aback.

'No, I'm not,' I laughed. But I was. I was watching money falling around Richard's face and it was making me feel good – pleased for Richard and Paula. The noise had returned to normal levels, my headache had gone. What I felt was . . . calm. A kind of peace, I suppose.

I don't want to see this anymore, I told myself. I don't want Richard in my head anymore, thank you. Obediently, the image disappeared and my mind was clear. Everything was clear.

'You'll be all right, love,' I repeated to Paula.

'Let's hope so,' she said, running a hand over her bump.

My eyes were damp and I took a sip of coffee. I knew she would be. I knew that she and Richard and their two kids were going to want for nothing. For the first time I was able to trust implicitly what I saw.

We had a nice coffee. Then, on the way home, I found myself going over and over what had just happened. I could ask for it to be there, I realized. I could ask for it to go away again.

Walking in the bright sun, pushing my pram through the cutting, I was thinking, *What if I try it now?* I summoned the image of Richard and the money, then banished it again. I was opening then closing myself.

It was like . . . how to explain? Like when you're a very small child and you're given a disappointing birthday present that you put in a drawer and forget about, only to come across it years later and appreciate it for what it is. Because you've grown up. Because you're ready for it now. It was like that with my gift. For years, no, for decades, I'd struggled with it, unable to explain it or understand it. It was an unwelcome, sometimes upsetting and painful presence in my head. It had got me into trouble. It got me called names and attracted sideways glances from people who didn't understand.

And all of a sudden those clouds had passed. I understood now. I welcomed it. I'd been able to see a comfortable financial future for Richard and Paula. I could see how it worked. That unwelcome present had finally come into its own.

'Oh, she does love looking in drawers.' Yes, mum, and look what I've found. Somewhere, I expect Nanny Gladys was looking down on me and smiling.

Later that night I said to John, 'I think I'm a medium, John.' Despite the spiritualists at Kelvedon Road and meeting Doris Stokes and years of seeing spirits and knowing things about people, I'd never thought of myself that way before.

'You what?' he said.

I used to think it was Waldemar behind it all. I'm not sure how, but I felt like it was the house that was somehow responsible. Plus mum had always drilled it into me: 'Oh, it was Waldemar that made you have all those funny things.' After that I'd associated it with other spirits. The man at Orbain Road. Poor old Mrs Walters. But after the events of that day I knew that I was a receiver. I knew what I was. It was like all those nights I spent beneath the bedclothes at Waldemar Avenue, transistor radio pressed to my ear trying to tune it. Straining for the sounds of chat and music to appear through the static. It was me. I was the radio.

There can't be many people who have had life-changing revelations in a Wimpy, but I'd had one that day.

'I'm a medium,' I told John.

'You look more like a large to me,' he said, then ducked to avoid the tea-towel I launched in his direction.

Cheeky bleeder, I was only about seven stone.

*

About eight weeks later, there was a knock at the door. I opened it to find Paula standing there. She'd had her baby in the meantime, of course, but she had other news, too.

'Can I come in?' she said. I made her a cup of tea and we sat at the kitchen table where she told me that Richard had fixed up some Rolls Royces in the street and got a bit of a name for himself doing it. He'd made a profit and had been able to raise the funds necessary to buy a garage. It was early days, but the signs were good.

'Our life's changed,' she said.

She looked at me long and hard across the kitchen table. 'That day in the Wimpy, when you said you thought we'd be all right?'

'Yes?'

'You *were* doing your thing, weren't you?'

'Yeah,' I said, 'I was.'

She became a great friend. Richard went on to become a multi-millionaire. Me, I'd learnt something about myself – about my ability. I could control it. Still, though, it seemed frustratingly random, like a skill that hadn't quite developed.

It's often said that a traumatic event can somehow shake loose things hidden inside of you. I'd be no different, and much, much sooner than I thought.

Nineteen

Remember how I always wanted to be a midwife? Always wanted to do something medical. When Fern was three years old, I went into general nursing at St George's Hospital in Tooting. The idea was that I'd study for my nursing exams, but fate got in the way.

It was July, two months before Fern's fourth birthday. We had the builders in. They were gutting the bathroom so the place was in a right state, with all sorts of kit on the upstairs landing, bags of cement and what have you. Also, we'd not long bought a bunk bed for the two youngest girls. I think Fern was on the bottom but you know how kids like to play on bunk beds. I'd be downstairs, hear the most almighty thump and it would sound like the ceiling was going to come in.

I would call, 'Hey, are you lot jumping off that bunk bed?'

I'd hear back, 'No, mum.'

'Then why does it sound like World War Three down here? Answer me that.'

Silence.

Kids, eh?

This particular morning it was hot. A hot summer's day. A Friday. John was at work, I was at home looking after the kids who were on school holidays, all apart from

Fern who hadn't started proper school yet; she came into the kitchen limping.

'What is it, darling?' I said, noticing. 'Have you hurt your foot?'

She was a tiny little thing. 'No,' she replied, tight-lipped, limping through the kitchen and out into the garden. I let her go, thinking, I'm not going to get the truth out of you, am I, madam? Then, wiping soap suds off my hands, I went upstairs to see the builder, Keith, and found him on the floor of the bathroom.

'My Fern hasn't tripped over one of your bags of cement, has she?' I asked him, indicating the bombsite on the landing behind me.

'Not that I know of, love,' he said.

'You haven't heard her fall off the bunk either? She's limping.'

'Not heard a thing, Sally, sorry,' he said.

Frowning, I turned and went back downstairs and into the kitchen where I stood at the window watching the three of them playing in the garden. Fern, though. Fern wasn't running around like the other two. She sat on the grass but when she stood to move, she was still limping.

Eventually I called her in and got her to sit at one of the kitchen tables where I examined her foot and ankle.

'You've hurt your foot, haven't you?'

'No,' she insisted. Voice small but insistent. Wanting to be back outside with the other two, not stuck inside with mummy. It's a sprain, I was thinking. She's jumped off the bunk and sprained her ankle. When I touched her ankle she was wincing. Definitely a sprain, I thought.

She wouldn't have it, though. Wouldn't come clean that she'd either tripped on the bombsite or tried a high-dive off the top bunk, and in the end I let her go back out to the garden, thinking, It'll heal. Nothing to worry about.

One load of housework later and I was bundling the kids into the car for a trip to Kingston. There were errands to run, the main one being a visit to the bank. If you've got kids you'll know it's not easy round town with three aged between four and ten. There are more pleasant ways of spending a morning, let's put it that way. They get bored, they act up.

Which is just what I thought Fern was doing when she fell to the floor of the bank, crying, clutching her leg, shouting, 'My leg, ow, my leg.'

Except it wasn't her ankle she was holding, writhing on the floor of the bank, as the other customers were turning to look our way. It was her hip.

'I thought it was your ankle that was hurting,' I said, crossly, hauling her to her feet, mortified, thinking, Bloody hell, she's just playing up. Attention-seeking.

'Come on you,' I said. And I made her stand. Then I made her trudge around Kingston with us as I got on with my errands. All the time she was complaining, holding her leg up near the hip.

The guilt I feel now, I can't tell you.

But she was still playing up, and I began to worry. And now she looked hot, so I ended up cutting the shopping trip short and taking the lot of them home, where I spoke to a friend of mine from up the road, Ann.

'Fern's not well, Ann, I'm taking her to the doctor's. You wouldn't keep an eye on my other two, would you?'

Fern was in less pain by the time we got to the surgery. Well, she'd been sitting so she wasn't putting so much weight on the leg, and when it got to the examination she seemed in less discomfort.

So when the doctor looked at me and said, 'We know what this needs, don't we, mummy? It needs a bandage,' doing all but winking at me, I didn't quibble. Why would I? He was the doctor. He knew best. It was a sprained ankle, he said, and who was I to say any different, with just a year or so of general nursing under my belt?

We got back to Beverley Way and I thanked Ann who went home.

Within about half an hour, the pain had got worse. Much, much worse. Fern was screaming. And if you've never heard your child – the most important thing in your life – screaming in pain, in *agony*, then thank your lucky stars. Pray you never have to.

'You've got to look after the kids,' I yelled at the builder, 'I'm taking her to hospital.'

Fern screaming. Perspiring. Tears of pain. Sweat on her face.

'But . . .' he said, 'I've got to go and . . .'
'*You ain't going anywhere.*'

He stayed, bless him, to look after the kids. Me and Fern, a mercy dash to the hospital. I sat her in the front, cursing every traffic light, every driver who dawdled at a junction, holding Fern's hand whenever I could, wiping the tears and sweat from her face.

She'd gone to bed a normal little girl. Now . . . No. Don't be stupid.

It was a break. It had to be a break. A break or a fracture. What else could it be? Which was what the doctor said. By now we were in a treatment area at Kingston Hospital, a curtain pulled around us. The doctor was trying to unwind the bandage from Fern's leg and she was still screaming, clenching my hand, red hot.

'Looks like a fracture of the ankle,' he said, wincing, trying to be as delicate as possible. My little Fern in so much pain. 'She'll need an X-ray.'

We took her to the X-ray department. She was still hot. Boiling hot. Still yelling out, the sound of it breaking my heart.

As a parent, you wish you could take that pain. You'd do anything – *anything* – to swap places.

They took an X-ray of the ankle. We returned to the treatment area and I was expecting to wait 10 or 20 minutes for the results of the X-ray, not just two, which is what it was before the doctor returned, a look on his face I'll never forget, but casting his eyes downwards, not wanting to meet mine; hiding something.

'We've got to X-ray the whole leg,' he said.

'What . . . Why?'

'It's . . . there could be . . . we need to check for any abnormalities.'

We went for a second X-ray. In the meantime, I'd called Ann and asked her to get in touch with John to let him know what was happening.

But before he could get to the hospital all hell broke

loose. Suddenly it was like every doctor in the place needed to see Fern. Doors were opening and closing. White-coated figures were everywhere.

'Mrs Morgan. Could you come with me, please? We'd like you to have a look at the X-rays.'

I found myself in a room with three doctors, me sitting, them standing, all of us looking at a lightbox on a wall.

'Fern doesn't have a fracture,' said one of the doctors, and he reached to fix an X-ray picture to the lightbox.

'What you can see here is Fern's leg. Can you see this shadow here, around the joint?'

I nodded, mouth dry.

'Right. Well . . .'

'Look,' I interrupted, 'what is it? Tell me. When can we go home?'

The doctors exchanged glances.

'Fern can't go home yet,' said the first doctor. 'She's very, very ill, Mrs Morgan.'

I suddenly had this feeling. Like a whooshing. Like a feeling of intense vertigo. Like I might be sick.

'Are you all right, Mrs Morgan?'

'Is she . . . will she be . . . ?' but the words wouldn't come. My dry mouth worked but the words wouldn't form.

'Mrs Morgan, I specialize in juvenile arthritis.'

My head swivelled to take in the second doctor. Thinking, *juvenile arthritis?* I'd done a paper on it as part of my training. Oh, I knew all about juvenile arthritis. I knew it meant the patient would spend the rest of their life in a wheelchair. And I started crying.

'She'll be in a wheelchair,' I sobbed into my hands.

'Whoa, whoa, what do you know about this?' said the first.

'I'm a nurse,' I told him, and their whole attitude changed; the atmosphere in the room changed. Suddenly they became much more businesslike.

'Right,' said the first, 'then I can tell you that we're doing bloods. We need to begin eliminating things and in the meantime all we can do is give her anti-inflammatories, but that's all until we know exactly what's wrong with her. I'm sorry – it's all we can do.'

John arrived. That night – Friday night – was one of the worst of my life and no doubt one of the worst of his, too. Fern's condition worsened. All night she lay suffering in so much pain, running a dangerously high temperature. A fan was pointing at her to try and cool her down. I wanted nothing more than to mop her face with a cool cloth but couldn't; she would scream in pain if she was touched. She was so sensitive to any movement that even touching the bed was agonizing for her. All we could do was be there for her.

Gradually the noise and hum of the hospital by day receded and night closed in. Lights in the ward dimmed but John and I barely noticed. We sat in plastic chairs by the side of Fern's bed. When we stood up the legs scraped on the tiles and the noise was like a bomb going off in the silent ward – silent apart from the whirring of the fan, the hushed voices of nursing staff regularly checking on Fern.

'The next two hours are crucial,' whispered a nurse to us.

We sat side by side and looked up at her, both mute with worry, watching her straighten, then walk away, soft shoes pad-padding on the tiles. I'm not sure if we ever actually found out what she meant. Something to do with medication. All we knew was that it was touch and go. Our daughter's was life hanging by a thread.

And the sound of Fern moaning, crying in pain, fluid – perspiration and tears – streaming off her. Me, her mother, unable even to comfort my little Fern. I sat on my hands to prevent myself reaching towards her. I held John's hand and fretted at my clothes.

'Why didn't I see this?' I asked John, late, late at night. My voice was a hoarse, exhausted whisper.

'Come on, love . . .'

We fell into silence. But, why? Why didn't I see it? Because I can't, don't, won't . . . what? Because it just doesn't work that way? Because I wasn't ready? Why can I see that so and so's boyfriend is having it off with the girl down the road? That so and so wants to join the army? Useless information I don't even want.

But not that my own daughter will end the day wracked with pain in a hospital bed?

Since that day at the Wimpy I'd started to think of myself as a medium; begun thinking of what I do as a 'gift'. Sitting in Kingston hospital in the dead of night, watching my little girl die, it didn't seem like any kind of gift worth having. What sort of bloody gift is that?

She drifted in and out of sleep. When she slept it was a release from the pain. If she was awake she was in agony. Hours later, she opened her eyes. Most of the time she didn't focus, but now she did, and our eyes met. She seemed to register me there for almost the first time since she'd been admitted and I drew my chair forward to speak to her.

'Fern? Fern, darling?'

'Please stop crying, mummy,' she said quietly. 'Please. You're upsetting me.'

She made it through the night. Thank you, God, for giving us that. The next day, Saturday, there was even more activity. More doctors came to see her, none of whom seemed to be able to agree what was wrong with her. A specialist on holiday in Cowes in the Isle of Wight had been recalled, we were told. He was on his way. In the meantime we sat, helpless, watching men in white coats bickering about what should be done with our little girl. It was as though John, Fern and I were still, frozen in time, statues around which the hospital revolved. Things had begun to take on an air of unreality. Nursing staff would speak to me and it would take several moments for their words to penetrate a fog of exhaustion and worry that permanently clouded my brain. John was the same.

One team of doctors thought it would be best for Fern to get up and try to walk around. Another doctor thought she should be turned. Nobody seemed to agree.

In the meantime the specialist had returned from the Isle of Wight. He'd driven back in full sailing gear and arrived at the hospital still with a white kerchief around his neck, dressed in navy and white.

He took John and me into the office, perching on the edge of his desk to talk to us. I suppose it was weird, surreal, maybe even funny to be sitting there speaking to this doctor in full sailing gear. But neither of us was laughing.

'I gather you've done some nursing,' he said to me.

'Yes.'

'Right, well, that's helpful, I won't pussyfoot around, then. Your daughter is one very poorly little girl.'

Somebody in the room let out a sob and I realized it was me. Sitting by my side, John grasped my hand.

'She's got one of two things. She's either got leukaemia, or she has a condition called osteomyelitis. Both affect the bone marrow. Both have similar symptoms at this stage and both are extremely serious,' he took a deep breath, looking from me to John. 'The thing is, if we treat her for leukaemia, we cannot then treat her for osteomyelitis. Not straight away. And if we treat her for osteomyelitis, the drugs we use for that would counteract the drugs for leukaemia. So you see the problem. We have to wait, I'm afraid, until we know for sure.'

I felt my shoulders drop.

'I'm sorry,' continued the specialist. 'I'm sorry the news isn't better.'

They gave her a massive dose of aspirin, hoping to bring her temperature down. We'd have an answer by the afternoon, we were told, but the afternoon came and still doctors were puzzled. There would be talk about blood cultures that I only half took in (always one eye on Fern who, despite the aspirin, was still dangerously hot, wracked with pain). They wanted to take her to Great

Ormond Street Hospital but didn't dare move her; the pain would have been too great. Instead, her blood would have to go for more tests.

The three of us sat, still frozen in time, the white coats whirling around us.

And then Fern began to complain of a pain in her bottom. Just four years old: 'Mummy, my bottom hurts. It hurts really bad,' and the specialist was summoned.

'We're going to have to turn her over,' he said.

My hands flew to my mouth. God, no. She couldn't stand it; couldn't take the pain.

'We'll give her a shot of pethidine,' he said, calming me. 'Mrs Morgan, we need to see what's there.'

They did it. They turned her over.

One of the cheeks of her bum was raised, almost into a dome shape.

'Okay,' said the specialist. 'I'm putting my money on osteomyelitis.' Once again he took us into the office. 'I want to treat her now,' he said. 'I want to treat her for osteomyelitis.'

Osteomyelitis, he told us: an infection of the bone marrow that spreads like wildfire throughout the body. It's rare in girls. Boys get it usually, from a contact injury. Rough and tumble. They pick up a bruise, it bleeds into the bone marrow and poisons it.

'Now, it could still come back from Great Ormond that she has leukaemia. In the final analysis it's up to you, but it's my recommendation that we treat her now and we treat her for osteomyelitis. Do you want some time to think it over?'

We looked at one another.

'No,' I said. 'Treat her now.'

They were right. That was what she had. Except plain, boring old normal osteomyelitis wasn't good enough for my Fern. No, she had to have it with complications. She had to have disseminated osteomyelitis.

Ann had a friend called Jenny, who had a son called Buffy. Fern used to love playing with Buffy and had been doing so on Thursday, the day before she was rushed to hospital. Falling from a slide she'd landed on her bottom and told Jenny, 'My bum really hurts, Jenny.' But that was the end of that. Only it wasn't, of course. The bump had caused a bruise which had bled into the bone marrow. At the same time, quite by coincidence, Fern had a throat bug, streptococcus. Now, if she hadn't had the osteomyelitis she would just have had a sore throat for a couple of days, but what happened was that the osteomyelitis had carried the streptococcus around the body. Fern was poisoning herself.

In the end, it was all in the timing. It got her just at the wrong age. It got her just when she had this throat bug. Then, of course, there was the bandage the doctor had applied (not his fault, he wasn't to know, and later he'd be in tears apologizing to me) which stopped the swelling, exacerbating the condition. Then there was me (and again, not exactly my fault, of course, but you have no idea about the guilt) dragging her around Kingston town centre that day. She'd developed pneumonia. She had Riegers Syndrome. And if all this sounds like a million-to-one chance, believe me, it was. They did a piece about it in *The Lancet*, it was that uncommon.

She was in hospital for 14 weeks. The treatment was intravenous but she was only four and after about 10 weeks her veins broke down. Teams of doctors would argue over how best to treat her. Sometimes John and I found ourselves transported back to that Friday night, helpless onlookers at our daughter's bedside as doctors once again bickered over how best to treat her. Should they turn her? Should they put her in a wheelchair? Etcetera, et-bloody-cetera.

We were approached by one in particular. He walked with a slight limp.

'I'd like to put her in traction,' he said.

I thought John was going to lose it: 'You people don't know what you're bloody doing.'

The doctor bowed his head in apology. 'Do you see my club foot?' he said. 'I had osteomyelitis when I was younger and that's what happened as a result. I don't want that to happen to your Fern.'

She ended up being in traction for almost the entire 14 weeks. Her muscles atrophied, her leg withered. When she came out of hospital she was in a wheelchair and for 18 months I nursed her back to health. I had to give up nursing as a result. When she was well enough to go back to school (although I say that, she's never *fully* recovered: even now, if she gets a sore throat it's serious cause for concern), I then found myself wanting to go back to work.

I'd changed, too. I'm not sure if I'd learnt anything as

Part Three

'I think I can help you'

Twenty

'Are you the lady who does readings?'

Standing there on the doorstep of my house on Beverley Way was a middle-aged, well-dressed Asian lady in a navy-blue trouser suit. It was one afternoon when I was at home looking after Fern – I heard the doorbell ring, opened the door and there she was. There was something intense about her. When she asked me that question she stared hard at me like she was desperate for me to be that lady, willing it to be me.

Traffic passed on the A3 nearby. I leaned out of the door and looked up and down the road. I'm not sure what I was expecting to see, but there was just a Mercedes parked at the kerb.

'Sorry, what do you mean?' I said.

'You're not the lady who can see things?' she pressed. Her hopeful smile faded slightly.

'Well, sort of . . .'

She clapped her hands together. 'You are. Oh, you are. I've been up and down,' she indicated along the road, 'knocking on people's doors, asking where the medium lives.'

My first thought was, *Oh my gawd, she's been telling the bloody neighbours I'm a medium.*

I mean, I knew the neighbours on either side, and

Alma was aware that I saw things, but it's not like I wanted the whole street thinking they had a witch living up the road.

'Oh, I'm sorry,' I said, 'I don't think . . .' I was about to close the door when I caught sight of the look in her eyes. A look of . . . oh, I'm not sure, but it was as if she was appealing with her eyes. As if by closing the door I was extinguishing her final hope.

'Please,' she said, seeing me hesitate. 'Please. I need help.'

I didn't need to think twice. I saw a woman sitting by a hospital bed, watching her daughter moan and writhe in pain, a nurse telling her that the next few hours were crucial. That woman was me. I needed help and was given it. So I could hardly turn my back on this lady, could I?

We walked along the hall and I gestured at the dining room table, where we both took a seat. Normally I would have shown a guest to the sofa, but I was still guarded; still wondering what she wanted and what she possibly thought I could do for her. Was I the lady who did readings? What, readings like Doris Stokes, sitting in her front room, nervous young dental nurses wanting to know who they were going to marry? That wasn't me. How did she find out about me anyway?

'I'm really not sure I can help you, love,' I said. 'I don't think I know what you want me to do.'

'Just try,' she said. Her hands were folded on the table in front of her. Her eyes were alive, dancing, and I saw in them a new look, one I've become so accustomed to since: hope.

'You can see things,' she said, 'Just tell me what you can see.'

Open sesame. I saw a man.

'You've come about your husband,' I said.

Details were jostling for attention in my head. Suddenly I understood all about this man who I knew was her husband; just knew it, the way you know your own name when you wake up in the morning. How he was a very vain man, incredibly fussy about his clothes. Oh, his looks were so important to him. I could see him preening himself in the mirror; could even see where he bought his clothes, which were tailored and immaculate. I saw into their lives together; saw that she was smart, too, and conscious of her appearance but nothing like her husband. She didn't have the ego he did. Or the vanity. Or the greed.

She nodded. The look she wore was half-gratitude, half-relief. But she said nothing else. Her mouth even tightened as though to show any expression would be betraying herself. (And you know what? I've seen that same look a thousand times since, over the years. When people come for readings they're testing you at the same time. Sceptics often say that psychics read body language. Well, that's rubbish. Let me tell you, most sitters are so tightly buttoned up it's like talking to a bloody waxwork.)

Then I saw someone else. A second Asian woman with longer hair than the lady sat opposite me. And I knew with that same certainty as before that this new lady wasn't a friend or a work colleague or a sister. This was his lover. He was lavishing presents on her. I didn't see him do it. Again, it was just a sudden knowing I had.

'Is he having an affair?' I said cautiously. I couldn't be sure. No, that's not right, I *was* sure. But I couldn't be certain whether it was the right thing to say. I'd blurted things in the past, of course, sometimes very unwisely (and to anyone who ever learnt anything they'd rather not have done, on account of me having 'too much of what the cat licks its arse with', then I'm truly sorry) but this was the first time I'd ever had someone come to me and *ask* me to see things. Was it right to tell her?

'Tell me more,' she said, simply.

'Look, I don't normally do this,' I said. 'I see ghosts and things, but this sort of stuff . . . I'm not sure I can do this.'

That appeal again in her eyes. 'Please,' she insisted. 'Please tell me more about my husband.'

So I did. I told her about the woman with long black hair. And the lady sitting opposite me nodded now; she knew the lover, obviously. And I told her how her husband was giving this other woman gifts, how they were together, and as a bit more than friends, if you know what I mean. That was about all I had to tell my visitor, but she nodded, satisfied. What I'd told her was no surprise. All I'd done was confirm something she already knew. She was pleased, though, I could tell. Not *happy*, obviously. Her husband was having it away with another woman. Just calmer, somehow; more settled.

'I want to pay you,' she said, as we stood.

'No,' I said, almost shocked. 'What you talking about? I don't want paying.'

There was a bit more chit-chat as I walked ahead of

her to the front door, where she asked me, 'Can I see you again?'

'Yeah, course, I'm usually here,' I said, and she left, climbing into her big Mercedes and driving away. When I went back through to the dining room I saw that she'd left a £20 note on the table, which was a lot of money back then. Especially for me, the long-term unemployed.

She did come back, too. That lady was not only my very first reading (I never did find out how she'd heard about me), she was my second, third, fourth and fifth. I never give out details of my readings so I won't divulge much more. Suffice to say, I was right. He was having an affair. She divorced him.

She also told a friend or two, because I began to do other readings, although I had to stop when John and I started our cleaning business.

Twenty-One

'Sally, could you do me a reading?'

This is one of the girls who worked at the laundry. Word had got round about my readings so they were forever pestering me for them. I suppose it was a bit of a perk of the job having a boss who was a psychic. More often than not I'd say yes, so we'd go out the back for five minutes or so.

I was in there one day when I heard the sirens. And hearing them I just knew – knew exactly what had happened. I knew because I'd had this feeling all morning . . .

But I'm getting ahead of myself. The laundry. It came about because we needed extra money and the kids were growing up. Well, it wasn't quite as simple as that – the way it actually began was because we wanted a holiday and we were, as they say, strapped for cash, so I was thinking of ideas to raise money.

You're probably wondering, 'Well what about the obvious one, Sally? The psychic bit? You'd already earned £20 from it.' To be honest it wasn't something I really thought of as a viable way of making money. I mean, it seems funny now, after everything I've done since, but I just wasn't thinking that way. It either didn't occur to me, or it did and I dismissed the idea. Instead, I went down to

Coomb Lane and put a postcard in the window of the Post Office, advertising my services as a cleaner. Calling myself Feather Dusters, I wrote, 'If you need a weekly clean, or even just a one-off spring clean, give us a call.'

Note the 'us'. A bit cheeky, really, because I was trying to make out there was an entire team of eager cleaners, when in fact it was just me and my Marigolds. I don't suppose I'm the first person to try that trick. Anyway, I'd barely been back from the Post Office five minutes when the phone went – it was my first customer. She needed some spring-cleaning, she said, and wanted to know how much did I charge? I'd literally just got back and she'd caught me on the hop, so I quoted her some ridiculous figure. As in, ridiculously low. It was £25, something like that.

Of course, I got there and she lived in a mansion, a huge eight-bedroom house that would probably be worth a couple of million these days. She and her husband were creative types and you know they are not exactly renowned for their cleanliness, those types. I'd say the house hadn't been cleaned for 20 or 30 years. They lived like a couple of dusty old Oxford dons.

But I cleaned it. I gave Gina a call, she helped and we split the earnings. After that I got another client, then another, until after three months I had a good little business going, mainly from word of mouth. Then I got a call from a letting agent, who managed loads of properties, and I ended up getting a contract for the lot. So now I started employing other cleaners. I put my duster away and took care of admin, while John became the company driver, ferrying cleaners around. From there we started doing the laundry for the flats, and after doing a deal with a local laundry we had the bright idea of opening our own.

'We can take passing trade,' I told John. We became very big very quickly. Which, looking back is one of the reasons everything went so badly wrong. That and the guy who ripped us off. But more of that later.

For a while it was great. We were doing well. We had the perfect life. Me, John and the kids at Beverley Way.

Then, something odd happened. In the late 1980s my mum and dad moved in next door.

'Old Mick's selling his house,' I'd told my mum one day. Some kind of uneasy truce had at least been established since I left home. By this time granddad had died and it was just the two of them, mum and dad, in the house at Waldemar Avenue – this huge, three-storey Edwardian home. Plus my mum had always wanted a garden, always. Hers had been taken up with dad's pigeons, that was the thing. No doubt she would have liked to sit in it and sunbathe or read a paper, but it wasn't exactly the most relaxing atmosphere. Instead, she'd come over to ours to sit in the sun.

It might even have been me who gave her the idea (foolish, Sally, really foolish), saying to my mum, 'You know what? You could sell Waldemar, buy old Mick's place and you'd still have a fortune left over.'

I wonder now why on earth I suggested it. Maybe because Jemma was spending so much time over at Waldemar that I thought if mum and dad lived next door,

I'd get to see more of her. She was always in Fulham, it seemed. Maybe I thought I could keep an eye on her if she was next door.

Maths has never been my strong suit but I was dead right about having money left over. They put Waldemar on the market and sold almost immediately. This was in the mid-80s, slap-bang in the middle of the housing boom. They made a fortune and, sure enough, they were able to buy Mick's place and move in next door to us on Beverley Way.

Mum wanted to move, but even so, she was in a terrible state the day they left. I went to help out and I remember, as we left it for what would be the very last time, sensing something inside the house, something that stirred. There was a darkness in that house, I always knew that. Waldemar was the source of so much that happened to me; it had shaped my life. Our family belonged to that house. It wasn't happy that we were leaving.

As we drove away from it, we glanced back to see a lorry arrive, a huge flat-bed piled high with cookers. The new owner was converting it into flats. It was to go from housing my mum and dad – *just* my mum and dad – to having 10 flats in it.

Now my mum and dad were living next door, and yes, I suppose I was getting to see a bit more of Jemma. Trouble was, if I saw her it'd be round at mum and dad's house. It was a bit like being in the middle of one of those ITV sitcoms from the 1980s: a weird, unrealistic family situation. And not funny.

But work was going brilliantly. The shop part of the

laundry was like a normal shop, but out the back it was a proper, industrial factory. We had irons, steamers, dry cleaning machines; the lot. It was in there that I used to give readings to the girls. In there that I had that feeling that morning, then heard the sirens.

The milkman hadn't been. He must have been about two hours late. Plus people coming into the shop were telling us that Fulham Road was gridlocked. You couldn't move down there they said. And there was this feeling I was getting, which was becoming stronger by the hour.

'Where's the bloody milkman?' grumbled John, in the office.

I looked at him, at last giving voice to this feeling that had been plaguing me all day.

'There's been a fire,' I told him.

'You what?'

'I know it. There's been a fire, John.'

'You sure, Sally? Where?'

'Yeah, I am sure, love. And I know where as well. It's Waldemar Avenue, John. Number 13 is burning down.'

I knew it. I knew just as surely as I know my house number.

John, who'd learnt to take me seriously when I had a feeling like this, led the way into the factory area where we had a television. The local news came on and the top story was a fire in progress in Fulham.

'Bloody hell, Sally,' said John, his voice hushed. The girls were gathering around to watch the news.

'It's Waldemar Avenue, John,' I repeated. 'Number 13.'

'You don't know that yet, love,' whispered John, but

moments later the milkman arrived, breathless and full of news.

'There's been a bloody great big fire down the other end of Fulham Road.'

'Waldemar Avenue?' I asked him.

'Yeah, love.'

'Number 13?'

'Well I wouldn't know about that. All I know is you can't bloody move out there.'

I jumped into the car but it was a pointless exercise. I couldn't get anywhere near Waldemar, the traffic was at a standstill. Instead I had to wait until the next day, when John and I took a drive over there and the whole way over I was thinking, *Please, God, let me be wrong this time. Please let me be wrong.*

I don't know why I thought that, I just did. All I knew was, I didn't want Waldemar to have burnt down. It was my house, I'd grown up there.

It's that spirit, I thought, as we drove. It's the spirit in the bathroom. What happens to them, I wondered, when their home burns down? Where do they go?

John and I were in the laundry van. Turning into Waldemar I caught myself leaning forward, craning my neck to see up the street, where number 13 seemed to stand out like a sore thumb.

It always did stand out to me, of course. But this was different. Now it was a smoke-blackened shell, a charcoal stain on the street. The area outside was littered with debris, presumably things saved from the flats: bits of furniture, a mattress, boxes, drawers, a television; all of it filthy and thick with smoke damage, the same colour as the windows and brickwork.

We stopped, killed the engine and I stared up at it, fighting tears. The old, proud house full of history, packed with stories. Only now it just stood there, empty and broken, gutted and hollow.

It was that spirit in the bathroom, I thought. It was you, wasn't it? I asked it silently.

Beside me, John let me mourn the house. My John, I can't tell you – he's full of humour, he's got a glint in his eye, but he's down to earth and pragmatic, too. He's the sort of man you want sitting beside you at a time like that.

'You all right, love?' he said into the silence of the van.

'Yeah,' I said, convincing nobody.

'How do you feel?' he asked, after another pause.

'Feel? I don't know. I feel like . . . like I've let the house down.'

'It wasn't your house anymore,' he said. 'Your mum had sold it.'

'It doesn't matter. It was our home.'

'Yeah,' he said, 'I know.'

I'm not sure if he really understood, though. How could he?

We drove away. There was worse to come, though. Later, we found out that a body had been discovered on the top floor, but it was never identified. We also learnt where the fire had started. I remember the sharp intake of breath when I was told. It had begun in the back bedroom on the ground floor. In my old bedroom.

Maybe I'm going to sound like a crackpot now, but I think the spirits in that house (or at least one of them) wanted it cleansed. It was like they were saying to us, If you don't want it, nobody's going to have it. And that's not just me, either. At one time or another everyone in the family has agreed on that. We left Waldemar Avenue and just a matter of weeks later, it was burning. Not that the fire ever really loosened the house's hold over me. That hold remains. I sometimes think Waldemar's the reason I do what I do. That, and what has happened to my family.

Twenty-Two

Things came to a terrible, terrible head at Christmas 1989.

And you know what? For a whole load of reasons, some of them personal and some of them legal, and because it's just so painful for certain members of my family, I don't feel able to talk about what happened, nor why it happened, nor really about the devastation it brought to my family. It's one of those things that must remain buried, known only to a select few who were there that day to witness it.

Suffice to say, we were due to go to Disneyland as a family, but shortly before we left for the airport – as in, the morning we were due to leave – it came out that something had been said. Just 'something'. I won't tell you what it was, or who said it to whom, but it was something that should not have come out. Not then. Not on the day we were due to leave for Disneyland on a family holiday.

The result of it all was that Jemma didn't join us for the family holiday.

I know, I know. That was how bad things had got. John, Fern, Rebecca and I went to Disneyland on what should have been the holiday of a lifetime, while Jemma stayed at home with my parents.

You can imagine what the holiday was like. We spent

a lot of time putting on a brave face. There was a lot of me sitting by myself on a beach while John took care of the children. John, bless him. He's no great fan of the water but that holiday he was often to be found with Fern and Rebecca at the water's edge while mummy stayed on the sand 'sunbathing', but really hiding crying eyes behind sunglasses.

We haven't exactly had the best of luck when it comes to going on holiday. What happened on the morning of the trip to Disneyland, well my family would never recover from that. And if I was to draw up some kind of graph of family problems, you'd see lots of spikes before and since, but that particular day? That day it really went off the chart. That day I lost a daughter and a mother. Or, at least, that was how it felt.

Returning from America, grimly trying to hold the family together, John and I soldiered on with the cleaning business. It continued to do well. It was doing so well that we decided to accept a once-in-a-lifetime safari holiday we'd been offered as part-payment by a client, leaving the business in the care of a man we'd taken on as a trusted partner. I can't name this guy for reasons you're probably already guessing. So let's just call him Pondlife.

Anther holiday memory I won't exactly savour. Excuse me if I don't get out the snaps to show you. How could so much go so wrong in such a short space of time? Because when we returned from that holiday we'd lost our business.

'Oh, you two go off and relax, you've earned it,' insisted

Pondlife, our trusted business partner, when we were dilly-dallying over whether we could afford three weeks away from the firm, 'I'll hold the fort here.'

Well, you've heard the expression 'being taken to the cleaners' . . .

He must have decided he was going to rip us off before we'd even stepped on the plane. The first thing he'd said to us was that he needed power of attorney while we were away, mainly because while we were out of the country the business was due to move premises. He was a trusted partner so we gave it to him (it's easy with the benefit of hindsight to be more suspicious, but the fact is we weren't; if you believe in someone then you believe in them, that's that).

So there we were, on our supposed holiday of a lifetime in Kenya. We decided to call home after the first week, only to be told by one of our employees that she couldn't get into the shop.

We started making more calls. We couldn't get hold of Pondlife. Nobody knew where he was. He was being trustworthy somewhere else, and as our holiday stopped being a holiday and started being a series of expensive long-distance phone calls each and every day, it became clear that wherever he was, he had all our money with him.

Oh my God, I can't tell you. The feeling: the feeling of being stuck out in Kenya, this beautiful, but let's face it, not exactly technologically advanced country, completely powerless over events back home. It's something I never want to feel again. We didn't have mobiles out there, of course. You'd have to book a call back home. And after that first call the news got progressively worse until we'd abandoned any last hope of enjoying the trip and were just trying to get home to save our business. Could we book earlier flights? No way. It was horrendous, absolutely horrendous. In the end we were just trying to console one another, telling each other, 'Come on, it can't be that bad. Pondlife's probably unwell or is detained doing something else.'

Then, because it never rains but it pours, I got ill after eating some ice cream that I'd expressly forbidden the children from touching because I was worried it might make them sick. Talk about do as I say, not as I do . . .

And of course we were wrong – wrong to be telling each other that it would be okay, and that Pondlife would turn up soon. Because it wasn't and he didn't. It transpired that he'd escaped with £90,000 of our money. When we eventually got back from Kenya we literally dumped our bags and John scooted straight over to Fulham and to the shop, but it was locked up. While we were away Pondlife was due to sign all the relevant paperwork for our building move. But he hadn't, of course, so the landlord had repossessed the property with all our stuff in it. And because of the move, the bank didn't query the sudden, unusual activity in our account. The upshot was that we lost everything, literally overnight. We had no money, no premises and all our machinery had mysteriously gone walkabout. When we left for Kenya we were happy and prosperous. We arrived back broke, desperate and, thanks to us giving Pondlife the power of attorney, helpless as well. The power we'd given him effectively made the money his. He'd said thank you very much and made off with it.

The holiday was a Christmas break. Yes, really. 'What did Santa bring you last year, Sally?' The family bust-up to end them all. 'Oh, nice, and this year?' This year I had all my money stolen and lost my business and my house.

Because it wasn't enough just to lose the business. We had a second mortgage on the house so we lost that, too. We hung on until June, but in the end we had to sell it back to the building society and move. We relocated to a flat in Pulborough for six months, then moved back to New Malden and lived in a flat above a greengrocer's where John worked. Our life was changing so quickly then. Bad luck followed more bad luck. As we were starting to get back on our feet, we moved into a rented house that we had an option to buy; we redecorated it with just that in mind. But the landlord took one look at what we'd done to the place and changed his mind. 'I can't sell this to you,' he said to us. Oh, he was as pleased as punch with what we'd done to his house. No way did he still want to sell it to us. It was like a hotel, he said. I thought my heart would break.

Even so, it was there, at the house in Worcester Park, where my life as a psychic took perhaps its biggest turn. I was working as a dental nurse part-time as well as seeing the odd person for readings. It still wasn't something I took especially seriously as a source of income. When we had Feather Dusters I often used to turn psychic clients away if they threatened to get too regular. I wanted to help them but if they kept coming back it would interfere with the business. It got to the stage where I'd have to develop codes with John to get rid of people out-staying their welcome, one of which involved him stamping on the floor of the bedroom for reasons best forgotten. Of course, the poor lady who'd come for the reading saw the lightshade move and thought it was the work of spirits – which only made her even keener.

But because I was seeing more and more people I could feel my skills growing stronger. My gift, like muscles you exercise, was developing.

Twenty-Three

These days, I wonder what was the start of it all, that gift? Was it Waldemar, the darkness of my childhood, the trauma of events with Fern, the problems with my mum and dad? I don't know. Writing this book I find I'm asking that question all of the time and hoping that when I come to the end my life will somehow make sense to me. Maybe that's asking too much, but we shall see. What I do know, though is that when I was able to focus on my ability it got better, it became stronger, and was getting stronger all the time. I would do readings for £25 an hour, and with each one, I was improving. Now we had our sights set firmly on buying a property of our own and I had contacts in what you might call the dentistry biz, so I went back to doing my dental nursing, part-time.

I was working with a dentist called Mr Carmax as his chair-side nurse. One day I was going through medical history with a patient: 'Do you have anything that could affect the heart, any history of rheumatoid arthritis?' when I had one of my feelings. I thought, 'She's got varicose veins in her throat.' And it was just like that. Somehow I just knew it. This lady had oesophageal varicea.

I asked to see Mr Carmax outside the room. 'You know, you're not going to believe this,' I told him, 'but

I'm a psychic. I'm a medium.' (I still wasn't used to calling myself that. Weird.)

'Er, right . . .' he said, no doubt thinking he was going to have to call the men in white coats.

'Well, the thing is,' I said, before he could make the call, 'I think she's got oesophageal varicea. I mean, I've taken her medical history and she hasn't said anything, but I think that's what she's got.'

It can be quite serious.

He glanced at the closed door of the treatment room. 'And you think this because you're a medium?'

'Yes.'

There was a pause, then he burst out laughing. 'Get out of it.'

'I'm sure of it,' I said. 'Honest. Go on, ask her. Will you ask her?'

He was a good man, Mr Carmax, and he nodded that yes, he would, and the pair of us trooped back into the treatment room where the patient sat waiting for us.

'Right,' said Mr Carmax to her, as we took our seats, 'we've got your medical history, have we?'

She nodded.

Mr Carmax and I exchanged a look behind her head.

'Excellent, excellent. And there's nothing you've forgotten?'

She shook her head.

We exchanged another look, Mr Carmax raising his eyebrows as if to say, 'Oh well.' I frowned back at him to try again. He rolled his eyes.

'Are you *absolutely* sure?' he pressed.

'Oh, I'm terribly sorry, I've just remembered,' she said. (We looked at each other, breath held.)

'I've been diagnosed with oesophageal varicea.'

Behind her head, I smiled at Mr Carmax. For his part, he looked shocked but gave me an 'I'm impressed' lift of the eyebrows.

But I was thinking, 'Wow,' because I could feel it getting so much stronger. I'd get these surges: *bam, bam, bam*. It seemed like every day I would get a little better at this.

It was while I was with Mr Carmax that I had an argument with his wife on the phone one evening. It was over a pay rise that I'd asked for that she didn't want me to have. Things became ... heated. I may have said something about taking a running jump. The next day I went into work when Mr Carmax asked me, 'What did you say to my wife last night?'

He already knew of course, and he sacked me. In those days you could just get rid of someone on the spot and that's exactly what he did. There I am, still acting the rebel, assuring him, 'Well, Mr Carmax, you've done me the biggest favour of my life, because I've just become a medium. As of now, I'm a medium.'

And I was. I told one of my regular clients I was going 'full-time' as it were, and I've never looked back, not once. I've never had to advertise, never even had a slow period. It just took off. One minute I'm a dental nurse, the next I'm Princess Diana's psychic. You couldn't make it up, could you?

Twenty-Four

Fast forward to Kingston University and, goodness, I'm telling you, this is where it starts to get really weird. This was so big for me. Another one of those life-changing chance encounters.

I was early, that's the first thing to say. If I'm ever late then there'll be a very good reason for it because I'm early for everything, and this was no exception. I honestly can't recall the exact circumstances of how I came to be invited, but I'd been asked along to give a demonstration, something I now know is called a 'platform event'. As I say, I know that now, but back then I was still wet behind the ears and this event was my very first one. So even though I wasn't nervous, mainly because I've never had any difficulty standing up and talking in front of people (talk to anyone, me – one or one thousand), I didn't really know the form. They'd be students in the audience, I knew that much, and accordingly, I dressed in leggings and a big baggy t-shirt, the height of fashion in the early 1990s. But otherwise, it was all a bit of a mystery to me.

Which was why, when I got there, I took a seat. I was so early they hadn't even put all of the chairs out, so I just plonked myself down in one to wait, and before I knew it they'd assembled an auditorium around me. Next, people were arriving and taking their seats, and I found myself in the middle of the audience, as it slowly dawned on me that I probably shouldn't be sitting where I was since I was supposed to be on stage. And bloody hell, there were a lot of people arriving, all to see me. How was I going to get out with all these people surrounding me? Imagine lying back to sunbathe and suddenly realizing the tide's come in. It felt a bit like that.

Well, maybe I actually was nervous, because instead of standing up and making my way to the end of the row, I sat tight, the audience now settled around me, all of them staring expectantly towards the front – where I was supposed to be standing.

Okay, I thought, I'll just wait here. Someone will come and get me.

The conversation in the hall gradually died down as people waited for the event to begin. Somebody coughed. I bit my lip.

Then, a woman appeared from somewhere at the front, coming out into the seated area and scanning the audience – obviously looking for me.

Rather sheepishly, I caught her eye.

'Are you Sally?' she said.

Everybody, and I mean everybody, swivelled to look at me.

'Yes,' I squeaked.

'Well,' she said, 'you're supposed to be at the . . .' She pointed towards the front.

'Oh,' I said, 'I don't want to make a fuss. I'll just come up when you're ready.'

She smiled politely, though no doubt thinking, 'We've got a right one here,' and made her way to the front.

'Right,' she said, addressing the audience, 'We've got a lady here who's going to give us a demonstration of her psychic ability. Can we have a warm welcome, please, for the medium Sally Morgan.'

There was an uncertain round of applause as I stood, saying, 'Excuse me,' to the young girl sitting next to me, and making my way to the end of the row, much standing up and shifting of knees as I did so.

'Hello everybody,' I said, when I eventually reached the front. For the first time I got a good look at them all. I'd been right to expect students, so the baggy t-shirt and leggings were the right decision. There must have been about 150 of them, all staring at me, this weird woman who'd emerged from the middle of the audience. They probably thought that was part of my act, which couldn't have been further from the truth, but it's funny, because my appearance from the audience like that was written about afterwards. I felt like a bit of a Charlie at the time, but it did me a favour in a way.

'I've come to see if I can see anything for you,' I told the audience. Most of them seemed to be in their twenties. These days I won't read for anyone under 21, and if any of this lot were younger than that, then they were borderline. But there was one young man seated in the front row who, I found out later, was 19. Immediately, I was drawn to him. It's something that has happened many times since and it's difficult to describe. It's as though I'm being gently pulled by invisible wires; as if I'm suddenly magnetized. It's a force – that's the only way to describe it – a force that coaxes me in a certain direction. It happens a lot in that kind of environment because I'm so open; I'm there doing my medium bit so I'm receiving. It's the same if I'm on tour. I have all this information in my head, all of it jostling for attention, and I scan the audience for a person to fit a piece of information.

(I find it quite difficult trying to explain it to you, if I'm honest. It's like trying to describe how music makes you feel, or what a delicious meal tastes like. In a way, it's just *there*. It defies description. Hopefully you have an idea anyway; perhaps you even know yourself.)

So here I was anyway, drawn towards this young lad in the front row. Beside him was his girlfriend, the two of them completely oblivious to the fact that my psychic Sally side was seeking them out.

I saw water first of all. It was as though the room was suddenly filled with water and I was viewing the auditorium through diving goggles; a fish even swam past my vision. And then, at the same time, I felt I had his mother with me. I didn't see her, though, not at first; I felt her there.

Now that's unusual. To feel the presence of a mother for such a young man. I looked at him. 'I feel as if I've got your mother here,' I said carefully, not wanting to get it wrong; not wanting to shock the poor kid. You have to be careful. It's like, if you see someone's got a dodgy heart, you don't just come right out and let them know they're at death's door. You say, 'Have you had your cholesterol checked lately? Well, you should.' You're talking about deeply personal things for people. Events that might be yet to happen. When you do a reading you're stepping into a person's life and you need to tread very, very gently.

He stared back at me, eyes widening a little as I pushed cautiously on. 'But why am I also seeing water? Are you a scuba diver?'

He shook his head no.

There was a titter from the audience. There often is when you get something wrong.

Or when they *think* you've got something wrong.

'But this is really strange,' I continued, 'because you'll never guess what? I've just had a fish swim past my eyes.'

Now there was a burst of laughter. I suppose it sounded quite funny the way I delivered it, and everybody laughed. All except this boy and his girlfriend, who just stared at me, their expressions telling me everything I needed to know. What happens at a time like that is . . . again it's so difficult to describe, but it's like an energy between me and that person. If I get what I call 'a hit', then that energy intensifies and more information comes.

And all at once I knew what it was I was seeing.

But careful with it, Sally, careful. This young boy. Oh, my heart was breaking for him even as I began to speak.

'I've got your mum here and she's in the water,' I said. The laughter in the auditorium died. 'Is she the reason you've come?'

He nodded, head bowing. I saw his girlfriend reach for his hand and squeeze it to reassure him.

Now I saw her, his mum. She was in the water and her arms were around a little boy and my first thought was, 'Oh my God, that's her son. She's under the water with her son.' But that thought was immediately replaced with a knowing that, no, that's not her son she's with.

'She drowned, didn't she?' I said.

He said nothing in response, fighting tears. Instead his girlfriend spoke for him.

'Yes, yes,' she said.

He didn't seem to be able to speak, the boy. Overcome, perhaps. Certainly the tears were rolling down his face. But now the image had altered slightly. Become murkier. The water was murkier. What I was seeing was deeper, deeper. I was at the bottom of the ocean and I could see a huge expanse of metal. What I realized, after a moment or so, was a boat.

'Oh my goodness, darling,' I blurted, 'did your mum die on a boat?'

He nodded. Members of the audience were craning their necks to see what was happening.

'He's nodded,' I said to the audience. 'He's saying yes.'

'Darling, I don't want to upset you, but was there someone else with your mother when she drowned?'

He nodded.

'Was it a little boy?'

Now he shook his head.

And I decided to take a risk.

'Well I tell you what, I've got your mum here. I can see her, and she's got her arms around a little boy. He's facing outwards. His head is to one side and your mum's holding onto him. Do you know who he is?

He shook his head no. Still he didn't make a sound. This poor boy, his girlfriend consoling him. Now I could hear a voice in my head. It was a man's voice and he was calling something, a name I couldn't make out. And in the next instant I knew who he was: her husband. He was the boy's father.

'Did your mum . . .' I stopped myself, not quite sure how to put it. An expectant silence hung heavy in the air of the room. Not a sound. Not a breeze. I barely needed to raise my voice above a whisper.

'Can I hear your dad there, too?'

His head was bowed. His girlfriend looked at me, her eyes confirming and I nodded 'Yes' at the audience. A muted gasp in response.

'Oh God, darling, please don't tell me they both drowned? Them and a little boy?'

I still didn't know the identity of the little boy. He was in the woman's arms. Was he another son, this lad's brother? No, I was certain not. Then who?

'They drowned together,' said his girlfriend as he nodded, but no, that wasn't right, it wasn't right. That's not what I was seeing. 'Wait a minute,' I said. 'Wait a minute, they weren't together.'

'They were,' he managed, at last. God, it was so quiet in that auditorium, the audience hanging on our every word. It was as though we were having a conversation across a kitchen table rather than talking in front of an audience.

But this wasn't what I was seeing. You have to be so careful, though. How could I tell him what I had going on in my head. This huge boat. I saw bits of bodies, arms and legs. Corpses that seemed to float, suspended in the water; sleeves, dresses billowing almost prettily in the sea; eyes of corpses open and unseeing, mouths gaping in a last scream or fruitless gasps for air. Everywhere, bodies. They weren't alone, his mum and dad, I was sure about that. But nor were they together. They were at opposite ends of the boat – I was certain of it.

I explained to him what I saw, omitting some of the more gory details.

'I believe your mum was at one end and your dad was at the other,' I told him.

'Maybe,' he said, barely managing to get the words out.

'Look,' I said, 'I'm under the water and I've got your mum and dad and a little boy you don't know. Can you tell us what happened? I think this is too important for me to talk about like this. Can you stand up and tell us? Are you able to talk about what happened?'

He tried to reply. So far he'd only said three words and he opened his mouth to speak now and nothing would come out. Unable to speak, so his girlfriend stood up and talked for him. She faced the front, addressing me.

His name was Johnny, she told me. His mother and father had both died in the Zeebrugge disaster, the *Herald of Free Enterprise* that overturned on March 6, 1987, killing 193 people.

'Oh, darling.' My hand went to my mouth. Johnny sat staring at the floor.

'Johnny,' I said. He raised his head slightly to look at me. 'Your mum, when she drowned, was holding a little boy,' I told him. His eyes were wet, tears streaming down his face. 'She was trying to protect him, or comfort him. I'm not sure exactly what, but she didn't pass over alone. I promise you she didn't pass over alone.'

That accident, well, they were still investigating it; still trying to piece together where passengers on the ferry had been when the boat capsized. Johnny had believed that his parents were together, in the restaurant area, but it wasn't what I saw, and it later emerged that his father had been in a different part of the boat, maybe on an errand.

His mother, it emerged, had died with a little boy, trying to protect him, or comfort him.

Speaking to Johnny, I felt something else, too. 'What's wrong with your throat, darling?' I asked him. That happens often. I get a sense of a person's ailment from doing a reading. He wasn't able to reply. Instead, his girlfriend spoke for him.

'He can't talk properly,' she told me. 'Ever since his mum and dad died, he has to carry a can of Coke to help him swallow, and the only way he can have a conversation is if he drinks from the can in between talking. Otherwise he can't swallow.'

I looked back at Johnny. 'Darling, that's grief,' I told him. 'You've got a ball of grief lodged in your throat and you need to get rid of that. I think . . . I think I can help you.'

After speaking to Johnny I went on to address the

meeting for over three hours, doing readings, answering questions, passing on messages. There was nothing quite so dramatic as the reading for Johnny, but then, there had never been anything as dramatic as that. Up until then I'd been reading for people wanting to contact relatives or find out if their husband was doing the dirty on them. I had a lot of clients wanting to know if they'd met Mr Right. Or if Mr Right was going to turn out to be Mr Wrong. Or if Mr Wrong might one day become a Mr Right, maybe with a bit of persuasion. I had people wanting to know if they should leave Job A and take Job B. Or should they threaten to take Job B in the hope that Job A offered them more money. These were – I hesitate to call them mundane, because it's all relative, isn't it? – but they were *everyday* problems. Johnny – Johnny was different. When his mum and dad died in the Zeebrugge disaster, he was orphaned. He was left wondering how they died. It had left him – literally – mute with grief.

I saw him, one to one, the very next day. Again, I saw his mother in spirit, and his father was there, too, and I was able to tell Johnny that his parents were together on the spirit plane. If there was any doubt in Johnny's mind that I was actually able to see his mum and dad, it went when I told him something his dad was unhappy about: his car. I passed the message on and Johnny instantly knew what I meant: his dad's car had been collected, then kept, by another family member. During that reading he managed to dislodge that ball of grief in his throat. Knowing that his mother and father were together in spirit helped Johnny deal with that anguish; he was able to talk properly again. No more problems swallowing. No more cans of Coke.

We've kept in touch and stayed friends. I really believe I helped him with some of the problems he had. In return he has helped me in more ways than he could ever know.

Twenty-Five

For Johnny, like a lot of the clients I've dealt with over the years, what he needed was to know that the spirits of his loved ones have remained with him.

I have my beliefs, of course, about spirits – where they are and what they're doing – and my beliefs are based mainly on my experience – experience gained, sometimes painfully, over decades as a medium.

But the thing is, I still consider myself a trainee when it comes to my gift. Slowly, over the years, it has revealed itself to me. These days, for example, I am able to see terrible, horrific things: murderers in the act; women being raped. See Johnny's mother in the water, arms around a child, both dead. As you can imagine, it's traumatic. But I didn't see those things, or anything like them, at four, five, six; Mrs Spooner on the stairs was about as gruesome as it got. Do you see what I mean? It's as though I've only been allowed to witness these things as I've become emotionally capable of dealing with them. This is why I think that some of the more distressing aspects of my life have helped me with my work. They've toughened me up; prepared me. I'll tell you what, I'm a sunny, bubbly person and what you see is what you get with me, but I'm a tough old bird, too; you underestimate me at your peril. Believe you me, I have to be tough. I have to be, just to deal with some of the stuff I have going on in my head.

I don't know how it happened, or what the formula is. Whether spirit world recognized that resilience and chose me; whether my life experiences made me the perfect candidate for the ability; whether it's just a chance-in-a-million combination of a person and events, but as I've grown, so has my gift, and still I'm struggling to understand it.

What I'm saying is, my thoughts on spirits are not definitive, not gospel; they're my beliefs based on what I've learnt from spirit world (or, to be more accurate, what the spirit world has shown me).

First of all, I believe that when we're talking about spirits, we're talking about a person's soul, and that it continues to exist long, long after the physical body has died, but on a different plane: the spirit plane, or spirit world. I see this soul as a ball of energy lodged in the body in the middle of your chest, the place where you feel sorrow and anguish and joy and love. When we die (I call it passing over) the soul moves from the earth plane to the spirit world, where it's drawn towards the living with whom they shared a connection. It's always a benign connection – I don't think I've ever met anyone with a person in spirit wishing them ill. Mainly spirits operate out of love, because if you ask me, love is the guiding force of the spirit world. I certainly like to think so anyway.

It's from a person's accompanying spirits that I'm able to see their future and past. Sometimes they tell me;

sometimes they show me. Here's where it gets a bit more complicated for me – where it can be a bewildering mix of messages, sounds, feelings and sensory input. I get glimpses of images. A person brushing their hair, knocking on a door, crying or laughing. Sometimes I might know exactly who that person is; other times I don't. I might hear snatches of speech. Often I get names. They can be quite indistinct at times: Paul can sound like Paula, Christina like Chris. But on other occasions they come through crystal clear and I'll blow people away by naming their dog or something equally impossible to just 'guess'.

Something else that tends to floor my clients is when I'm given something physical by spirit world. I had a client once who had lost her mother and came to me in order to try and contact her. Many, *many* of my bookings come from the bereaved hoping to contact a lost loved one. I mean, I've done plenty of other work, too, like helping with addictions, seeing health problems, financial issues and, well, pretty much anything you can think of, but the vast majority has involved bereavement. With this particular woman, I was relaying messages from her to her dead mother and vice versa when something quite strange happened.

'Why do I want to do this,' I said, and I was playing with my index finger, just the top part of it.

'Oh my God,' she said, hand to her chest. 'That's my mother. My mother's here.'

'Well, yeah,' I said. 'Who do you think I've been talking to all this time? The whole reading's been with your mum, sweetheart.'

'No,' she said, breathlessly, 'but that really *is* my mum. Her whole life she had a problem with that part of her finger.'

And from that moment on, she was looking at me in a totally new light. Now, what on earth had been going through her mind before the finger bit, I wouldn't like to say. She was paying her money for an hour's reading just like anybody else. She'd been agreeing that I was talking to her mother and dabbing wet eyes with a hanky. But was it only when I began playing with my index finger that she *really* believed? I'm not sure; I can't know exactly what's going through my clients' minds when they're sitting opposite me. But I do have a theory: even for those who believe in my work, their belief is never absolute. By which I mean, there's a safety mechanism in there somehow; something in their mind that stops them truly believing. Otherwise, how could they leave? Countless times I've had difficulty getting rid of clients; as I've said, I've had to develop all sorts of strategies with John for 'gently' getting them to leave. But if I'd lost someone and I thought some psychic in New Malden was the only one who could speak to that person, I'd want to stick with them. You've seen the film *Ghost*? I suppose it's a bit like that.

I don't know, I can't say for sure, but I think that even those who think they believe must have something deep inside that allows them to walk away. Doubt? Fear?

Perhaps – and I really hope this is true – it's just enough for people to know that the spirit is there with them; that they take comfort from that. Around the same time as the finger lady, a guy came to the door to make an appointment. He'd recently lost his wife and was hoping to contact her, although he wasn't expecting it to be there and then. Opening the door to him, who should I see in spirit with him but his wife? Frowning, concerned, worried about him, so intense was his grieving.

'It's okay, I know why you're here,' I told him and invited him in.

'Tell him Pam is here,' the spirit was saying, and my visitor almost lost his footing, the shock of hearing her name on my lips knocking him for six. His wife was worried about him, she said, because he didn't go home, and he nodded, agreeing that he couldn't face the house without her. Her absence was too much for him to bear. Instead he was spending time with his sister. Pam, though, was worried about this; she felt it was important he was at home and that while it might be hard he'd eventually take comfort from being among their things.

He was nodding. Did he believe? Did he really believe I was speaking to his Pam?

'She says you have to go home, love,' I told him. 'She says she misses you in the kitchen.'

He knew then; he understood. He buried his face in his hands and began to cry. As is so often the case the message I relayed meant zilch to me yet meant *everything* to the person I was giving it to.

When he left, he was able to go back home and over-come whatever difficulties he'd had in the house. Why? Well, I believe it's because he was comforted by the presence of his wife's spirit. Just as with Johnny or the

lady whose mother had the funny finger, it was knowing
the spirit was there that helped. Not thinking, but knowing. One other story to illustrate what I'm talking about:
two sisters came to me hoping to resolve some guilt issues
over the death of their father. The pair of them had
emigrated to Australia and soon after they left, their father
died. For various reasons they didn't return to the UK for
about a year after his death, when the two of them visited
his grave. Instantly they were overcome with guilt. They'd
deserted him, they felt. They should have been with him.
They came to see me in an attempt to work it out.

'He was with you when he died,' I told them, listening
to his spirit.

'I'm sorry?' said one of the ladies.

'He was watching you that day.'

I saw their body language change, their mouths tighten
as though preparing to give me a dressing down. I mean,
I knew what it sounded like to them: as though I was
simply telling them what they wanted to hear.

'With us?' said those distrustful expressions. 'How
could he be with us?'

'He saw what you did that day,' I said.

And I could see it too. I saw them that day. I heard
the chatter of the kitchen, children's' voices. Through me
their father described their movements that day. I saw
their mouths drop open as I told them things about their
lives that had happened over a year ago and thousands
of miles away.

Things I couldn't possibly have known. And neither
could their father – unless he'd been with them in spirit.

Twenty-Six

The two sisters from Australia had been distraught with guilt when they decided to visit me, but they went away reassured. The spirit of their dead father had wanted to help them, and I'm convinced that that's what the spirit world wants to do – help people on the earth plane. Which is why I never get malicious messages.

Maybe it's another part of the weird equation I'm talking about. The spirit world saw in me a person who wanted to help other people and knew I could be used in that way. Sounds a bit fanciful, I suppose. Either way, I am committed to helping those on the earth plane, and it's one of my golden rules that I won't tell someone if I foresee their death. I've had plenty of people ask me about it in the past; I've even had clients visit me having been spooked by another medium, and I'm pleased to say I've been able to put some minds at rest. But generally speaking, if it's an untimely demise I'm seeing, I keep it to myself. And spirit world knows I'll do that; I wouldn't be shown it otherwise. I'm given this information for reasons of full disclosure but there's a bond of trust between me and that plane. For the same reason, I'm extremely careful when revealing the details of deaths. Like I say, spirit world gives me the full works but only because it knows I'm capable of dealing with it myself, and because it can trust me to be sensitive with the details when speaking to the client.

I'll give you an example. I had a father ring me one day, telling me about his teenage son who had been due to go to university. Suddenly, just talking to the guy on the phone, I found it difficult to breathe. I had the feeling of being stuck in a small space and there was a strong smell – a smell of oil.

'I can sense him here,' I told the man. There was a pause. He cleared his throat, not sure whether to believe or not. Wanting to believe. Oh, I knew that all right. He wanted to believe his son was with me.

'He's telling me something,' I said.

'What? What is he saying?'

'He wants me to tell you that he's pleased he was able to look normal in his coffin.'

I heard him catch his breath at the other end of the line. And whatever that meant, he knew – he knew his son was with me.

He continued with his story. His son had been working on a farm, a summer job before he began his university career – what should have been the happiest, most joyful years of his life. But there was an accident. The boy had been cleaning out a fuel tank and another farm worker started up a tractor nearby. The tank had gone up in flames, burning the boy who was dragged out of the inferno and laid on the ground outside. He'd been up a ladder and because of the way he'd been standing his front was virtually untouched. That was why he was able to look normal in his coffin. His back, though, it had been horribly burnt. So badly that he died very shortly afterwards.

Yet somehow he'd accepted his death; was even able to try and help his father come to terms with it.

'How could I have lain in bed, dad?' he asked, through me. Again, it was one of those messages that didn't mean a lot to me. Some kind of family in-joke, perhaps? Whatever it was, his father confirmed how important it was.

Another time, I was in New York. This was a lot later, after 9/11 when I spent a lot of time over there talking to and counselling relatives of the victims of the attack. While there, I walked into an apartment for a reading and instantly had the feeling of being shoved backwards. It completely took me by surprise, and almost knocked me off my feet.

I stood there for a second trying to regain my composure, staring around at a roomful of people, all of them no doubt thinking, 'We've got a right one here.' My gaze settled on a man sitting in an armchair.

On his shoulder I could see a spirit – a baby. Straight away I knew it was his son and I was trying to piece things together in my head, trying to get the information to make sense. The baby, the feeling of being thrown backwards.

But no, there was another presence. This was his wife.

I went towards him.

'Why can I feel this presence around you?' I asked, pulling up a chair and placing myself in front of him, oblivious, for a moment, to the other people in the room.

But they all knew, of course, what I was about to learn:

that his wife had been killed. That she was pregnant at the time.

It was a startling reading. This man, he broke down as I gave him messages from his wife. She wanted him to know that she was all right and that their son was there with her. The baby knew all about his father, she told him, saying, 'Don't ever think you were not a dad – because you were. But now you've got to move on with your life. You know why? Because if you don't, then my killer hasn't killed two people – he's killed three.'

She asked me to tell him to stand up and he did. I turned, asking him to put his hand on my shoulder blade. As he did so, we knew that it wasn't me he was touching, it was her.

That was a moment when emotions went off the scale, which is so often the case with readings where children are involved. As I've said, one of my rules is that I won't read for anybody under 21. But so many of my readings *involve* children. Lots are to do with children to come, and over the years I've had heaps of clients come to me for pregnancy predictions because not only can I see if someone's going to have a baby (I get a lot of career women who've left it late to have a kid wanting to know if they can conceive), but when. I was chatting to a lady at a party and I told her I saw a baby in her future.

'Ridiculous,' was the retort. After all, she was 48.

The next time I saw her, she was 51, and I saw the baby. 'You're expecting, aren't you?' I told her.

'Don't be so silly,' came the reply. She'd known me long enough to know better, though, which is no doubt why she looked uneasy, admitting, if she was absolutely honest, that she had been feeling slightly unwell and looking warily at the glass of wine in her hand.

'Best enjoy that while you can, darling,' I told her. 'You won't be having many of those for the next nine months or so.'

And you know what I'm going to say, don't you? That's right, she had a little girl. At 52 years old. She and her husband were pleased as punch.

I told another client on her very first visit that she'd end up having twins, a boy and a girl, and she poo-poohed the idea. No way, she said. She and her husband were into their careers, going out and having a good time, and kids were the last thing on their minds. Some years later and guess what? They have children. Twins, if you please, a boy and a girl.

Something that ended up making the papers happened in the early 1990s – shortly after the meeting at Kingston University, in fact. Leigh Robinson, from Windsor, came to see me to try and talk to her grandmother in spirit. I was able to reach the grandmother who gave me some interesting predictions about Leigh's children. At the time she had one, Alex, a three-year-old boy. However, I saw another child in her future. This one, I said, would show huge interest in a particular subject and he should be encouraged to do so. I could see the boy holding some kind of cup or trophy, standing on grass. A decade or so later and young James is a rising star on the youth tennis circuit, having been sponsored to attend an academy in Italy.

Alex, meanwhile . . . well, I was able to see something

for him, too. To Leigh I said, 'He'll spend his life in front of the camera,' a prediction they all, no doubt, promptly forgot about until at 15 he told them he wanted to be an actor. Next thing you know he was playing Tom Brown alongside Stephen Fry on telly. Needless to say it wasn't long before Leigh was back in my office, having remembered my prediction about her son spending his life in front of the camera. Did I see anything else in his future, she wanted to know?

I did. Hollywood beckoned for Alex, I told her. I could see him playing a spy in a major film and his career would go from strength to strength.

The next thing I heard was that young Alex had won a leading role in *Stormbreaker* alongside Ewan McGregor and Mickey Rourke.

These are some of examples of the nice things I'm able to see about kids. But something I often get asked – and it crops up during readings and on tour – is what happens to the spirits of miscarried babies. It's strange because I really don't have many (or any) answers about that. One more thing about my ability that I'm trying to make sense of as I go along, I suppose.

Sometimes I see the spirits of miscarried babies and they are so tiny. Goodness, it is so emotional. I've had so many clients break down over the years over spirits of babies they've lost; so many times I've gone up to that kitchen to boil the kettle in their wake, fighting back the tears. I'm a mother myself. I don't know what it's like to lose a child (like that, anyway, although I think of my Jemma and wonder if I've got a better understanding than most), but I pray I never find out. Sometimes the baby spirits I see seem to have grown, and are the age they should have been, had they lived. I've seen baby spirits that at first appear to have no connection to my client but later turn out to be a baby miscarried by their mother. The answer is, there is no answer, but this I do know: to all the women who have ever been through a miscarriage, that baby is in spirit, I promise. It is with you.

For almost 20 years I've been a professional psychic. During that time I've dealt with so much stuff – certainly more than would ever fit in a single book. I've built up a loyal client base, starting with the Asian lady who was a well-known, prominent person, and who gave my name to other people, which then, by word of mouth, led to more people coming to my door. I've never had to advertise; never needed to tout for work. I've been lucky also because my name became known in what you might call high-fallutin' circles. It wasn't long before I was reading for some pretty high-ranking people. Over the years I've read for captains of industry, for politicians, TV and sports stars, film stars, you name it. I actually met one lady who introduced me to many people in those circles that first night at Kingston University. She is a writer called Brenda Juretic who, it turned out, I'd been sitting next to before I made my way to the front.

'You were phenomenal,' she said. 'Tell me, did you know that boy?'

Johnny, she meant. And no, I assured her, I'd never clapped eyes on him before.

'Well that was amazing,' she said. 'I've never seen anything like it.'

She was bowled over, obviously, and wanted to write a piece about me. Not only that, but she wanted to know whether I would be interested in participating in something she did: MICE, which stood for Meetings in Industry for Charity Events. For me, this was huge. Brenda was as good as her word and she wrote a very complimentary article about me, plus I did some of her charity events. She was a very well-connected lady, who lived in a posh mansion block in North London and introduced me to some high-rolling people who lived there. As a result of my association with her I began attracting, well, I guess the only way of saying it is a higher class of clientele.

If only I'd known then how high class. One day, she gave me a call.

'I've got someone I'd really like you to meet, she's quite important,' she said.

I said, 'Sure.' I was used to her saying stuff like that by then.

'Can we meet in Kensington?'

'Yeah, of course.'

Twenty-Seven

I met Brenda outside Kensington Garden Hotel one afternoon. Just after lunch I think it was.

By the side of the hotel there is a little alleyway. It's not that big really, but it leads down into Kensington Gardens.

'So,' I said. 'Who is it I'm supposed to be meeting?'

She fixed me with a look. Traffic passed: BMWs, Mercedes . . . this was Kensington High Street. You could almost smell the money in the air.

'Look,' she said, 'I couldn't tell you before, and you mustn't tell anyone, it's a friend of mine from Liverpool, but the secret thing is who she works for. She's got a very important boss.'

'Okay,' I said, still none the wiser. Still not putting two and two together, because why would I? Brenda had already introduced me to a lot of people she described as important. And if I'm absolutely honest, 'important' is a bit of a relative term, isn't it? After all, one person's 'important' is another person's 'the wife of the boss of some company I've never heard of'.

They may be important in their world, is what I'm saying, but not necessarily in mine. To me, 'important' was my John, my girls.

'It's this way,' said Brenda.

At first I thought we were walking towards a back entrance to the hotel. I'd done events with Brenda there, so I knew it. But we weren't. Instead we arrived at a sentry box. Me, I was wondering what's she up to, then, and I was looking around, thinking this had to be some kind of joke, when Brenda approached the policeman at the sentry box, had a word, and he stepped out of the box and raised a barrier. Letting us through, he smiled politely, telling us he needed to accompany us round the back – we went around the side of a huge building that I was about to discover was the home of the Princess of Wales.

(Ah, that's what you mean by 'important'.)

And when I say apartments, I mean that's what they're called: 'the Princess of Wales's apartments', but they're not like any kind of apartments you and I have ever seen. Bloody great big house, mansion, *palace*. That's more like it.

And that's what it was. It was the palace. *Kensington Palace.* Stepping back there, let me tell you, is like walking through some storybook door into another world. One second you're right in the heart of London, the city swirling around you, all its familiar sights and sounds and smells; the next it's as though you're in the country, at a country estate.

Here in the courtyard not only was it like a different place, but it was like a different time as well. Back in the olden days. The surface was gravel but even so, I half expected to hear horses' hooves on cobblestones. There was a sense of tranquillity, of order. Did I feel it because of what I can do? Because I was over-awed? Or just because that's exactly how it is? I wasn't sure then and I'm not sure now. But it was gorgeous, absolutely beautiful. I remember there being hanging baskets everywhere and there was a large door, beautifully painted and decorated with stained glass, that I later discovered was the Princess of Wales' front door. *Her front door.* At this point, 1992, she was estranged from the Prince of Wales and lived there full-time. I wondered whether she was inside. Would I find out?

Opposite her door was a row of mews apartments. These were for the staff. They were like little country cottages. Once upon a time they had stables beneath and to get to the front doors you had to climb a short flight of steps, which we did now, to meet Brenda's friend.

Now, I can't say the name of Brenda's friend, so let's just call her Carol. She was a youngish woman, very smartly dressed. She wore a smart white blouse, pressed navy trousers. Throughout the whole time I knew her she was never less than immaculately presented. She always looked so clean and crisp. Lovely hair framing a peaches-and-cream complexion. She had to look good: she worked at Kensington Palace. And I was to do her a reading.

Brenda left and the reading with Carol began. About halfway through it her phone rang and she answered it, listening for a moment before saying, 'No, your shoes are on the lawn.'

A beautiful little apartment, it was, and as I say, it was so quiet it was like being in the country. I'm no eavesdropper believe you me (do you think I need to?)

but I could clearly hear who was on the other end of the phone. No doubt about it – it was the boss.

'Will they be ready?' asked the Princess of Wales at the other end of the line.

'I'm sure. They're drying now. I've dyed them and they're on the lawn drying.'

Goodness, I thought, Princess Diana dyes her shoes. Well, we've all done it. Mind you, most of us don't have maids to do it for us, but still . . .

'Yes, they're identical,' Carol was saying. 'The colour's identical to the dress, don't worry, it's all done, they'll be ready for you tonight.'

Next, I heard the voice on the other end of the line ask, 'Is she there?'

Oh my God, she's talking about me, I thought. Carol winked at me, knowing I'd heard.

'Yes, she's here,' she replied, grinning. 'No, she won't be too much longer now. Yes, of course I will. All right, bye.'

She put the phone down. 'That was one of my bosses,' she said.

Funny, she never actually said it was the Princess. I mean, I knew it was her. After all, we were in Kensington Palace. And she knew I knew it was her. But whether it was deliberate or not, Carol never confirmed it to me. That was my first little taste of the mystery and secrecy and sometimes outright paranoia that seems to surround the Royal Family, and certainly the Princess of Wales.

'Really?' I said. 'That was her?'

'Yes, I've just dyed some shoes for her. I sometimes

help her out with things. She's panicking that they won't be dry, but I've left them on the lawn so they should be okay.' I glanced out of the window, a beautiful summer's afternoon. The Princess of Wales's shoes would be dry in no time.

'And she knows I'm here?'

'Oh my goodness, yes. She knows everything. She knows you're coming, she knew you were here. I've had to fight for her not to come over.'

'Oh my God,' I said, almost screaming it, but thinking, Why? Why can't she come over? By that time I already had some really high profile clients, but the Princess of Wales . . . if you can't be a little bit star-struck by the Princess of Wales then I don't know what. Of course I wanted to meet her.

'Oh, she loves people like you. I think that she wants me to let you know that she's . . . interested in you.'

'Really?'

'Yes. Listen, do you fancy a cup of tea?' said Carol, rising from her seat, and I followed her into a cute little apartment kitchen with a pretty outlook. But immediately my eye was drawn to something on the side: a milk bottle. Ah, but no ordinary milk bottle. This one was a *Royal* milk bottle. All other milk bottles are mere plebs compared to this one, which had a sleeker, taller shape, and bore the Royal crest. Like a lot of ladies I sort of collect kitchen memorabilia. I especially like stuff from the 1950s. It's nice to have it on a windowsill, isn't it? So as soon as I picked up this milk bottle for a closer look I was coveting it.

'Oh, what a lovely bottle,' I was cooing, just as the phone went again.

Carol answered, and was listening. 'Yes, yes I've told her,' she was saying. 'She knows who you are. She's just admiring one of your milk bottles now.'

Carol came off the phone and wandered back into the kitchen, gesturing at the milk bottle. 'She says you can have it,' she said. 'Here, I'll wash it out for you.'

Oh, it's one of my most precious souvenirs that milk bottle. I keep a red rose in it.

'She's itching to come over,' said Carol.

'I can stay . . .' I offered. All casual like.

'No, no, you don't want to stay. She'll never let you go.' Perhaps my face fell a little. Maybe Carol realized that even if the Princess of Wales was one of her ultimate bosses, and like any boss you want to take a break from them, she wasn't my boss. I didn't want to take a break from her (maybe later, but we'll come to that). I was just an ordinary woman, well, an ordinary psychic, anyway. I would have loved to do a reading for the Princess of Wales.

'You'd be happy to see her, then, if she wanted to?' said Carol, as I was leaving. We were standing in the hallway of her flat.

'That would be fine,' I said. 'Of course.'

'Do you see anything around her now at all?'

Looking back, was this a test? Was it all part of a big test? Was I being vetted to see if I was the real deal? Well, I am, so bring it on, and I did see something around the

Princess, yes. It was Carol saying it. It was like, *bang*. Did I see something? And instantly, I did.

'I see the initial O,' I said.

Carol's face registered nothing.

'It's a man. He's a tall man and she's got to be very careful of him, he's going to cause her trouble. And there's another initial, too. It's H. the initials OH are what I see.'

Still, Carol's face displayed nothing. Looking back, I wonder if she knew. Did she know the letters stood for Oliver Hoare? After all, she was a very close aide of the Princess and she would have been privy to details of her private life: some that would never be made public; some that wouldn't come to light until much later – details of relationships she was having, for example.

I left with Brenda and we parted ways so I could get the train home. All the way back I was thinking, 'I've just been to Kensington Palace. Princess Diana was asking about me.' All the way back I was clutching the milk bottle in my handbag, absolutely paranoid some commuter was going to bash into my bag and break it. All the way back I was thinking, 'How am I going to tell John? Am I even allowed to tell John?' Everybody's so bloody secretive, after all. About an hour after I got home, I remember it was around six in the evening, the phone rang, and it was Carol.

We exchanged pleasantries. She said how much she'd enjoyed the reading and asked me to clarify a couple of points, but I could sense it was just chit-chat and that we were leading up to the main event.

Sure enough: 'The boss would like you to do a reading for her.'

I almost gasped. 'What? You mean the . . .'

'Yes.'

Always 'the boss', never the name. She told me later that they had to refer to her as Your Royal Highness first thing in the morning. Like if you had to wake her up in the morning, take her a cup of tea, open her curtains, whatever, then you said, 'Good morning, Your Royal Highness,' but that was the only time you had to use her full title. The rest of the time it was ma'am, or, more informally, 'boss'. And among the Kensington Palace staff, just 'the boss'. As I became more familiar with the workings of the household over the years I realized that the Princess ran a tight ship. I guess like most members of the public I had this image of her as being, I don't know, a bit more informal and laid-back than the rest of them. If you'd asked me, I might have said I imagined her being 'friends' with her staff, for example. But it wasn't the case. Yes, she was serene and quite relaxed but even so, there was an importance about her, too. There was no being friends with her. Put it this way, there was never ever a moment in the four years I dealt with her that I wasn't wholly aware I was speaking to a member of the Royal Family.

'You want me to read for the boss?' I repeated.

'Yes.'

'Okay. How? When?'

'I'll tell you what I'll do,' she said. 'I'll come over. What do you need?'

'Well, if she's not in front of me, then I'll need something very personal to her. A watch or an item of clothing. Plus I'll need her to write down everything she wants to know.'

They must have been checking me out. Well, they'd have been foolish not to. I may have looked like your average London psychic housewife but I could have been a highly trained assassin. There must have been security checks; I'm sure that Carol's visit was a part of all that.

The house she came to was the one we were doing up, Brookside Crescent. At that time we still thought we were going to buy it. Isn't it weird? Professionally, things were going super-nova. I was about to do a reading for the Princess of Wales. Personally, it couldn't have been worse. I hardly spoke to my daughter; we'd lost our business and we were about to get double-crossed on the house by our Nigerian landlord.

On the one hand, a royal client. On the other, royally shafted.

Anyway, Carol came over. She drove herself and arrived at the front door clutching a little green Harrods carrier bag. I took her into the kitchen, made tea, and we got seated opposite one another at the table.

From the bag she took something swaddled in a piece of cloth, placing it on the table and unwrapping it. A gold watch. Beautiful. I picked it up. Heavy. On the reverse was engraved the Prince of Wales' feathers.

'Oh, look,' I said to Carol.

'It was a gift from Prince Charles,' she confirmed.

Next she took a pair of socks from the bag. Nike gym socks.

'Don't worry, Sally,' laughed Carol, 'they're clean. I checked with the person who does all her little bits and pieces.'

Now she placed something else on the table: a piece of headed notepaper. On it were about 15 to 20 questions.

It wouldn't be right to tell you what they all were, of course. Besides, I can't remember (Carol took the piece of paper back with her), but many of them were the usual things any woman would want to know about her family. She wanted to know whether the boys were happy, for example. Then there was the question I was to hear from her a lot over the time we were in contact: Will I be Queen? She wanted to know about somebody called Barry. Was Barry in spirit? she wanted to know. And will I find happiness with OH?

We started the tape running and I reached for her watch. It's a good thing to hold, someone's watch, because usually it sits on their pulse and I can work with that a lot. I'm not sure exactly what it is, but I remember as a little girl that if I caught sight of someone's carotid artery – you know the vein in the neck – and it was pulsing, I would start to get things. Still, it's not like I *need* a watch as I can do telephone readings with no prompts at all, and would, many times, for the Princess of Wales, but it helps, and if somebody offers to bring something along, then I always accept.

Her father was there. I saw her father, Earl Spencer, and knew right there and then I'd seen the root of her emotional problems. Here was something I knew and understood only too well. Growing up she'd experienced distance and coldness from her father. Her parents had separated, which was something she desperately wanted to avoid for herself and her children. Latterly, her father had shown her affection, but it was too little too late. That childhood experience had left her vulnerable, needy and craving love. But what had happened? She'd married a man just like her father. She ached for Charles to give her the love she needed but instead, he broke her heart. Totally, totally broke her to pieces. Like a lamb to the slaughter she went, brimming with the fairy-tale of it all. And then, even though they were separated, she was still having difficulty accepting it. Charles was the first man she truly, truly loved and that was no small thing to her; that meant a lot. Old-fashioned in a way, traditional, she was the kind of woman who felt that once she had a man's children, he was the man for her and she would stick by him. With Charles and the boys she wanted normality. She wanted the family for her boys that she hadn't had as a child and Charles took that away from her. Still, she hadn't quite accepted it though; the penny hadn't dropped. Still she was living a lie. There's no nice way of saying it, but the Princess of Wales was living in la-la land. On the one hand she desperately wanted to be with Charles. On the other hand she had people within the system telling her, 'You can still have everything. You can still go to functions with Charles and we'll let the world know you're together, and then he'll go home to Camilla and you'll go home to Kensington Palace.' But she didn't want to go home to an empty apartment in Kensington Palace. No matter how luxurious and glamorous and opulent her life was she didn't want that. She was attractive and she knew it. Men were attracted to her. Why should she go home to an empty apartment? She deserved more. So she was torn – torn between wanting back the love she once shared with Charles and spreading her wings as a woman. Torn and unhappy.

All of that I saw, just by holding her watch.

'You know,' I told Carol, 'I can only be honest. I'm not going to make anything up. I mean, just because she's the Princess of Wales. She has to have it like anyone else.'

'That's how she'd want it,' said Carol. 'She'd insist on that. Can we have a look at the questions?'

I wasn't sure what I could say in front of Carol, so I didn't tell her that I knew this OH (I found out his identity along with everybody else, in the tabloids) was the Princess's lover.

'This OH,' I said. 'It'll only bring tears if she continues to have him around.'

I could see that she was romantically involved with several men. And I tell you what, over the years I began to realize that a lot of what went on in the tabloids, well, you know how celebrities always like to say that it's all lies? It certainly wasn't lies where the Princess of Wales was concerned. Most of the stuff I saw in the tabloids between 1992 when I first became involved with the Princess and 1997, when she died, was spot on. It was the broadsheets who got it wrong. Sitting there, grasping her watch, though, I knew this OH wasn't the one for her, and that it would go spectacularly wrong. It did, of course.

Would she be Queen? I'm afraid I saw the answer was no. Easy for me to say in retrospect, of course, but I knew it then; I was absolutely certain about it. As I say, it was one of the Princess's recurring questions. I used to say to John (my one and only confidant) that the Princess would never be Queen and he used to scoff because he knows all about politics and stuff like that: 'Charles can't divorce Diana,' he used to say, 'the Prince of Wales can't get a bloomin' divorce.'

'I'm telling you, John, she ain't going to be Queen. It's just not going to happen.'

'Nah . . .'

He just didn't believe it. The Princess of Wales, on the other hand, just didn't *want* to believe it. On that first occasion, however, I told her (well, via Carol and the tape and my scribbles on her page of questions) that she wasn't with the Prince of Wales, so how could she be Queen? And that I didn't see it in her immediate future. In subsequent readings it would always provide me with a sticky moment, that particular question. She would often go very quiet. I did a lot of telephone readings with her over the years and I grew used to the silences during those moments. I never told her what I told John, of course. That would have been cruel. I simply informed her that I couldn't see it in her future. And I couldn't. Quite the reverse.

Barry. I had to say I couldn't see him. I'd be hearing a bit more about Barry in the months to come. This was Barry Mannakee, a member of her security team. She was rumoured to have had an affair with him and then he died in a car accident. Later it became clear to me that she didn't believe it was an accident, but at that time she just wanted to know if I could see him in spirit, and I couldn't.

By the end of the reading I felt as though all of the answers I had for the Princess were negative. As I told Carol, I couldn't tart up what I saw, even if it was for Royalty. And this happens an awful lot in my work. I get a lot of clients who come, not to hear the truth, but to have certain assumptions or beliefs reinforced, and they can get quite – how shall I put this? – 'dissatisfied' (oh, all right, just plain old arsey) when they don't hear what they've come to hear. That's when they go away thinking I'm not what I say I am. It happens every now and then. From my office I watch a client walk to their car wearing a disgruntled look on their face and it's because I haven't told them what they wanted to hear. Not much I can do about it. Apart from hope that in the future what I've said will make sense to them. The penny will drop.

So with this in mind I told Carol, just as we were saying goodbye, 'She's not going to like anything I've told her. She won't come back.'

She held the little green Harrods bag. In it were the gold watch, gym socks, her tape and the piece of paper with the Princess's questions and, now, some of my scribbled answers.

'Oh, don't be silly,' she said, 'you'll be hearing from her.' And off she went.

She wasn't wrong.

About three hours later the phone rang and it was Carol. My girls were in bed asleep by now; John in the house somewhere, pottering about.

'Hi Sally.'

'Oh, hello.'

'Look, I know it's really late, but is there any chance the boss could speak to you?'

'What, now?'

'Yes. I'm sorry. I know it's late, but . . .'

'No, it's not that . . .' because it wasn't that late. Getting on for ten pm. I'd have to get used to dealing with late-night calls as it turned out anyway; the Princess liked to call at all hours, she was a telephone junkie, I'm sure of it. 'It's just . . . she wants to speak to me *now*?'

'Yes.'

It was turning into quite a day.

'Er . . .' Madly, I found myself wondering how I looked. How weird is that? 'Okay,' I managed, pulling myself together. 'Put her on.'

'No, Sally, it doesn't work like that.'

And so began what would become a familiar routine. The phone rings and it's an aide telling me that the next time the phone rings it will be the Princess of Wales.

'I'm going to put the phone down. Keep the line clear, please, and you'll get a call and it'll be her. Is that okay?'

'Yes.'

(Oh. My. God.)

'Okay, Sally, bye.'

Click.

I put the phone back on its cradle.

In those days our phone was in the hallway on a little table. No seat or anything. Like everyone else in the world we'd go phone mad in the next few years or so and we'd have mobiles and a portable phone in the house. But not just then. We made our arrangements and that was it.

I stared at the phone now. Plastic thing. Sitting there not doing anything. Mad thoughts were going through my head: what if I hadn't placed it back on the cradle properly and the Princess tried but got the engaged signal? What if someone else in the house picked up the extension right now? What if the phone rang and it wasn't her but some mate of John's? What on earth would I say to get them off the line in time for . . . ?

The phone rang.

I picked it up. 'Hello?'

'Sally.'

Not a mate of John's. Not a friend of Rebecca or Fern. It was her, the Princess of Wales.

'Sally, this is so kind of you to speak to me so late. Thank you so much for allowing Carol to come over earlier and for all the lovely things you've said.'

She sounded exactly as you'd expect her to. A soothing tone. Slightly breathy.

'What would you like me to call you?' I asked her. For some reason I was preoccupied by this. I mean, I didn't have to call her anything, really, did I?

'What would you like to call me?' she said.

'Pardon?' I blurted, caught off guard. *What would I like to call her?*

'You can call me Diana,' she said next.

'Oh I don't think I can call you that,' I said. Again, I'm really not quite sure why I said that. I guess I was as flustered and off-guard as anybody else would be if the Princess of Wales called them. Imagine the most excruciating social situation you've ever been in then multiply it by ten. That was what I had to deal with at that moment.

'Well, think of a name,' she said. 'How about Mary. Would you like to call me Mary?'

'Well,' I said, 'not really,' and for some reason I thought, *This isn't going to work. I can't do this.*

'Well we won't worry about that,' she said. 'Really, we don't have to call one another anything. Whatever – whatever you feel like, Sally.'

I never, ever called her Diana. All the years I knew her I don't think I used her name once. I called her Ma'am a few times, but I'm not even sure I was pronouncing it correctly: I rhymed it with jam. What I'm saying is, from that moment on I never worried about protocol. It was just never an issue. Which, for me, was lucky, because you know what I'm like. I like a bit of a rabbit. Even if you're the Princess of Wales. So next I was going off on one about how I was sorry I didn't have any good news for her, but she was telling me that it was okay, not to worry, then asking me about my family.

'Are you married, Sally? Do you have children?' She was used to putting people at ease – doing the whole Royal bit.

But here's the thing. Standing in my hall, swapping pleasantries, knowing she was doing her best to relax me, I realized – in both a psychic and just a plain logical sense – that this was a woman who needed answers. Assuming Carol had gone straight back to Kensington Palace, she'd only been back an hour or two – enough time for the Princess to listen to her tape. She'd rung me virtually straight away. Certainly we were going through this little dance where the Princess calms the commoner's nerves and all that, but to put it in slightly base terms: she was dead keen. She was *desperate* for answers.

That night what she wanted to know most about was this OH. She didn't say his name and, as I say, I still didn't know it then. Still, though, I could only tell her what I knew: that I thought this OH was bad for her; that he would bring her unhappiness. Again, she asked about being Queen. Once more I told her what I thought, although as before I was 'selective' with the truth. What I'm saying is, I did my best to let her down gently.

Of all my clients – I'm talking ever – I think I was probably the most careful with her. Not because I wanted her to come back; that was never in doubt as far as I was concerned. More because it was obvious to me that the Princess was in a bad place; that she needed direction and comfort and hope in her life, and that coming out and telling her, 'No, love, you're never gonna be Queen, sorry, Charlie loves Camilla and that's it,' wasn't exactly going to do the trick. And also because I was aware that what I said might have far-reaching consequences.

We went through the list of questions and I virtually

repeated what I'd already said on the tape; then, at the close of the conversation, she said, 'It's been so good of you to speak to me, I really hope I haven't interfered with your family life. Would it be all right if I called you again?'

Of course it would, I told her. And I knew then: she's going to become obsessed. Knew it.

I put down the phone and ran in to see John. 'Ohmygod, ohmygod, you'll never guess who that was on the phone?'

'Was it Princess Diana?'

'Smart arse. Yes, it was.'

He was in front of the telly watching football or whatever. Normally he can't drag his eyes away from the footie but now he looked at me. 'Bloody hell, Sally.'

Even though John knew I was in daily contact with her for those four years I never told him what we discussed. Not once. Some of it I'm saying now for the first time.

Anyway, I flopped down onto the sofa beside him, staring at the TV but not really seeing it. It had been quite a day, that much was for sure. I started it as plain old Sally. I'd ended it as psychic to the Princess of Wales. Nothing would ever be quite the same again.

Twenty-Eight

The next day I had a phone call from Carol: 'Would it be okay if the boss spoke to you again?'

She'd got me between clients, midday, it was. So, yes, it was fine. I put the phone down and waited for the call . . .

'Thank you so much for talking to me.' Oh, she was always so polite. And concerned, too, that she might be interrupting my family in some way; she'd often ask about them or express concern that her phone calls were some kind of intrusion. It was as though she idealized my family life. If only she'd known the truth . . .

Once again she wanted to run through her shopping list of questions. Why, I'm really not sure. Perhaps she'd been dwelling on them overnight. Maybe she'd discussed with friends or confidantes (I was learning that the Princess of Wales spent her life talking on the phone), whatever. All I know is she wanted me to reiterate or clarify some of the points. I don't know, maybe it was some kind of test. She wanted to see if I was consistent. Was I still being evaluated? A psychic on appraisal. Perhaps so, because the next thing I knew I was being hauled back to Kensington Palace, after a call from Carol, who wanted me to do a reading for some 'friends of the boss'.

I agreed and a few days later John drove me to Kensington Palace one evening.

On arrival, we gave our names and were allowed through the barrier. We were expected, you see, and John drove around the side and into the courtyard between the Princess's apartments and the staff mews, where he stopped the car. From nowhere, a policeman appeared, bending to the driver's window, which John opened.

'Good evening, sir,' said the policeman. Everybody at the palace was always incredibly polite. It really is exactly as you'd expect it to be. They knew full well where I was going, as they have all this sort of stuff written on the clipboards that they carry, and they knew it was 'only' to the staff quarters. But still they were always unfailingly courteous. It's quite comforting really.

The policeman explained that we weren't allowed to leave the car in the courtyard, and I suspect it wasn't just because we were lowering the tone. He was about to tell us where we could leave the car when John suggested he go back home and return for me later if I gave him a call when I was done. Fine, said the policeman and I got out of the car, kissing John goodbye and watching him drive out of the courtyard.

My John. Bless him. He'd go home and deal with the girls. We were doing some decorating at the time, so he'd get a bit of painting done while waiting for my call, then return to collect me.

Meanwhile, I was shown to a room. Not one of the staff apartments, but what I can only describe as a meet-and-greet room, furnished like a very comfortable sitting room with a lovely thick carpet, fireplaces; all the original features. And there waiting for me was a whole room of some of the most well-groomed and well-bred ladies it has ever been my fortune to meet. They were ladies-in-waiting. I think there was a hair stylist or two as well, possibly even a colour specialist. I don't know exactly, but I do know that these were very important people in the Princess's entourage and I was to do readings for them all. This, I soon realized, was another test. Fair enough, I suppose. I know that as a psychic you are *always* being tested. Every reading is a test; everything you say is scrutinized, and that's fine. Whether someone believes in a psychic or not affects how they feel about some pretty major issues: life and death and destiny, maybe even God and religion. People with brains question the world around them, and I'm lucky, I don't deal with stupid people, so it stands to reason that I'm going to get questioned, occasionally treated with hesitancy and distrust and, yes, tested. Even by the Princess of Wales. So far I'd done a reading for Carol, but Carol I knew through Brenda, so as a test subject she wasn't that reliable. I'd done a reading for the Princess herself, but she was one of the – if not *the* – world's most talked-about women (probably still is) so that was hardly 'cold'. No, she wanted readings for people I couldn't possibly have known about; couldn't have read up on beforehand. All I'd been told before stepping into that room that night was that I was to read for some friends of the boss. It could have been Elton John for all I knew.

I was there all night. Reading after reading for these

immaculate, very, very posh ladies. I was in a side room doing one at a time while most of them were in the main room.

When it came to the final reading I called John, so that by the time I'd finished I left my little ante-room and walked out into the main sitting room to find him waiting for me.

Oh my gawd, I almost died. The state of him. Sitting there, giving me the most sheepish look you can possibly imagine, surrounded by Royal ladies-in-waiting, he looked like something the cat had dragged in. His hair was sticking up all over the place. He wore paint-splattered jogging bottoms and an old, paint-streaked t-shirt, and he was unshaven and baggy-eyed.

I stared at him. My smile freezing. He knew full well that if we hadn't been in company I'd have gone ballistic at him. Tell you what, he should count his lucky stars he had all these ladies-in-waiting cooing all over him bringing him tea and coffee.

'I'm sorry,' he said, 'I fell asleep.'

Later, he told me that he'd put on his decorating clothes to do a bit of work, taken a 'little break' and promptly fallen asleep on the sofa. Woken up by the phone calling him back to Kensington Palace he'd assumed he wouldn't even have to get out of the car once he arrived, so he drove straight over without bothering to spruce himself up. Of course, once he arrived he was shown through to the courtyard and settled down to wait but the polite policeman had come knocking again: 'Excuse me, sir, I'm afraid I can't allow you to wait in your vehicle. You'll have to go and wait for your wife up there.'

So, looking like a cross between Wurzel Gummidge and an accident with a tin of Dulux he trooped up to this room to wait for me.

We laugh about it now, of course. But at the time . . .

'I heard about your husband,' chuckled the Princess the next day. I must have passed her test with flying colours because the following morning Carol called. Would it be okay to speak to the boss? Of course, and moments later I was hearing from the Princess about my husband falling asleep on the sofa. She knew the whole story.

Then it was down to business. For the first time she referred to this OH by his name. Not his full name, but she called him Oliver. And she was very keen to know as much as possible about this relationship. I told her that I saw a townhouse, a very tall townhouse somewhere in London, and I recall thinking to myself how odd it was. What would the Princess of Wales be doing in a townhouse, because even though it was a white, Eaton Square-type townhouse and probably worth a fortune, it still wasn't exactly a palace, you know. But I could see her walking around it, as though she was planning to buy it, and I told her so.

There was a pause from her end. She couldn't believe it, she said. What I was telling her. Did I see anything else?

'Yes,' I said, 'he'll let you down at the last minute.'

Not long after that, I read in the tabloids about a man with whom the Princess had had an affair. An antiques dealer called Oliver Hoare. Diana told me she'd been looking at houses in Belgravia. She wanted to move in with him. It was to be – for want of a better word – a lovenest. It never happened. As is common knowledge, the relationship with Oliver fizzled out. I'd been spot on when I'd said that OH would only bring the Princess tears. Apparently, she'd cried her heart out when the relationship ended.

That was the beginning of it. From then on, the Princess would call me often. Usually Carol would call beforehand, although there was the odd occasion when the Princess would call directly. The first time it happened, who should pick up the phone but Fern? She didn't realize it was her at first, which was why, instead of coming to get me she did that typical teenager thing of slamming the phone down on the telephone table and bawling at the top of her voice, 'Mum! There's a Diana on the phone.'

But I bet the Princess loved that. I think I would have done in her shoes. Thirty seconds of normality. A tiny moment in the day when she wasn't *Princess* Diana. She was just a woman on the phone called Diana.

It soon became clear that the Princess was talking about me in Royal circles because I had a visit from a lady-in-waiting to the Queen Mother – a lady in her 70s, dressed in navy blue, a blouse with a frill on the collar and – like all of them – immaculately turned out. I used to wonder how they managed to stay so clean, so unruffled. Something in the genes, I think. Then there was another lady, Wendy, who had been a housekeeper at Highgrove.

'Oh,' I said, 'you've written something, haven't you? And it's going to cause you a lot of trouble.'

Turned out she'd written a book, *The Housekeeper's Diary*. And perhaps it was because of that – all this Highgrove stuff surrounding her – but from her I picked up lots of things about life at Highgrove. How a burglar alarm kept going off, for example, which always summoned the police within seconds. But with Wendy was a man called Paddy.

'Paddy?' she said.

'Yes and his wife's here, too. How weird is this? She's called Mrs Paddy.'

'Well, that's right,' confirmed Wendy. 'Paddy was the Prince of Wales's right-hand man at Highgrove and his wife was Mrs Paddy. They used to walk Highgrove.'

'Well they do it still,' I told her. 'They're on the stairs at Highgrove and that's why the burglar alarm keeps going off.'

Next I told her she was going to America, which blew her away because she hadn't told anybody, not even her son. She had to stay there in the end because of the book, just to escape prosecution. Prince Charles took out an injunction against it.

The next thing to happen was that the Princess wanted to see me.

Often it's the other way around. I see a client first, and then I do telephone readings for them. Nine times out of ten the readings are just as effective over the phone as they are face to face. People often like to think that it'll be a better reading if we do it in person; they have even insisted upon it (as if they know), but the fact is, it doesn't make a massive amount of difference to me. But many people believe that face-to-face equals more accuracy, and the Princess of Wales was no different. So one day she asked me if I was going to be in town the following morning. I'd go to Kensington and Chelsea a lot, doing readings for wealthy clients, and she wanted to know if I could 'pop in' while I was about. You know, I'm sure I would have popped in whether I was in town or not, it being the Princess of Wales and everything, but anyway, we set a time and along I went.

Once again I found myself talking to the policeman at the gate, only this time I was on foot, and alone. He walked me round. It was now a familiar route. Onto the gravel, around to the courtyard with her apartments one side, the staff quarters on the other. Except this time I wasn't going to see the staff. He took me to that front door, that huge, beautiful front door with the stained glass in the window which, as we approached, seemed to open as though electronically commanded. There stood a member of staff, black suit, white shirt.

'Hello, Mrs Morgan, this way please.'

My police escort seemed to fade away behind me, and now I was following this man who led me into a hallway, like the hallway of a large country house, with flagstones on the floor. We reached a set of carpeted stairs, big, but not grand – not *quite* the kind of stairs you might imagine, I suppose – and climbed them to a landing where he ushered me into a drawing room.

Inside, beside a sofa near the fireplace, stood the Princess of Wales. I glanced around the room. There was a piano, and there were lots of pictures on the wall – photographs and watercolours. I half expected to see one, huge imposing portrait, perhaps with eyes that might follow you around the room, but it was mainly smaller pictures – and plenty of them. Not that I had much time to take it all in because the Princess was stepping forward to greet me and showing me to a chair, also beside the fireplace.

She looked beautiful, of course. I don't doubt for a second that she got up in the morning and looked a right state like everybody else in the world, but the Princess I saw at Kensington Palace was as stylish and radiant as ever she looked in the papers, on the red carpet, in public life.

But what the pictures and film never quite fully conveyed was her charisma. Partly they did, certainly. That was why the British public fell so utterly, head over heels in love with her. But in the flesh? When you met her this warmth seemed to roll off her. She was one of those people who speak with their eyes. She had these huge, wide eyes. Famous for them, of course. But there was so much soul in those eyes. When I think back on her, I think that's the main thing she brought to the Royal Family; what they've struggled with ever since. Everybody talks about how she brought glamour to the Royals and of course that's true. I mean, she was *gorgeous*. But looks were only part of it. No, what she really brought to the Royals was soul. I'm sure of it.

She thanked me for coming, as always. And then the reading began. I sat opposite her. The room where we did it was the same room where the interview with Martin Bashir was conducted for *Panorama*.

'Who's Paul?' I remember asking her.

'Oh, that's my butler,' she replied. I now know him to be Paul Burrell, of course. His wife, Maria, was one of those well-bred and well-groomed ladies-in-waiting I'd read for a few nights previously.

'Oh, he's going to hurt his back,' I said. 'You must tell him not to lift that piano,' indicating the piano in the room.

The next day there was a photoshoot in that room and Paul Burrell was helping to move the piano. Guess what happened? He put his back out. When I next spoke to the Princess she couldn't get over it; it blew her mind that I'd predicted that. She told me, 'I screamed and said, "Sally predicted that."'

(And if you're thinking, Well if Sally could predict Paul Burrell doing his back in trying to shift a piano, why couldn't she foresee the death of the Princess, well, I'm coming to that.)

It lasted around an hour, our face-to-face reading. During that time she wanted to know about the usual things: her love life, her boys, Prince Charles. She wanted to know about Barry, and told me a little more about him. He'd been a member of her security staff and she thought very fondly of him. If you look him up nowadays he's often referred to as being one of her affairs or flings, though it's generally accepted that things never got particularly serious or physical. However, he'd died in an accident that would end up having weird similarities to the accident in which she died.

What the Princess wanted to know was whether the crash that killed Barry had been an accident. I told her I didn't think so. I wasn't sure – and I'm still not – how it happened, or who was responsible, which is what I told her.

She wanted to know about divorce, too.

The thing was, she never wanted a divorce. Her own parents had this horrible, messy, played-out-in-the-courts divorce and she just didn't want that for herself, poor love. She still hankered after Charles and she quizzed me about him: 'Why?' she said, leaning forward, looking at me with those wide, wide eyes. 'Why did he do it?'

It wasn't on that occasion, but one time on the phone we were talking about Charles and she was doing what she always did, which was to press me on why. Why, why, why?

I used to try and change the subject because I'd already given her the answer. The fact was, she didn't need a psychic to give her the answer. It was because he was in love with somebody else, pure and simple. He had loved her, that I knew. And I can tell you that Prince Charles never intended to break Diana's heart. He did love her. The trouble was that in the end he loved Camilla more, pure and simple.

'Well, what sort of women does he like?' she asked me one day.

'Well I tell you what, he loves a bust,' I said.

Actually, I'm fibbing to you. What I actually said to the Princess of Wales was – and I can't believe I said this to her – 'Well I tell you what, he does love a pair of tits.'

She roared with laughter.

Two days later there was a photograph of her with the Prince. I think they were at a sports day for the boys. She was pictured by a large oak tree and all the talk in the press was of the dress she wore: a tight, cotton dress that accentuated her cleavage.

For some time the go-between in my relationship with the Princess was Carol. It was she who had first organized it and she who used to arrange the payment. The Princess paid just like any other client, no more no less. The only difference between her and a normal client was that I used to arrange things directly; John, who usually dealt with bookings, didn't get involved at all. Otherwise, she paid her £35 an hour as any usual client would. I was always paid in cash and always on time either by Carol at the beginning of my dealings with her, or, latterly, by another person I'll call Fiona. Now I didn't know this Fiona was connected to the Princess until she brought it up, and it was then that she took over the job of go-between. As with Carol she'd pay me cash, literally from her purse. I remember on one visit she was rooting around in her handbag and me saying, 'Don't worry, you can pay me on the next visit if it helps.'

'Oh, it's in here somewhere,' she replied, 'I know, because I've just got my family allowance out.'

How the other half live, eh?

One day, shortly after we'd moved into our new home in New Malden, where we've stayed ever since, I was doing a reading for Fiona in one of the bedrooms. What often used to happen was that I'd do a reading for Fiona, during which she'd ask about the Princess. Fiona would then take the tape back to Kensington Palace. There would be a gap of a couple of hours or so – no doubt the time it took the two of them to listen to the tape – then the phone would ring and it would be the Princess wanting things clarifying or explaining. I'd hear Fiona in the background, too, the pair of them giggling. But this particular time, oh, the bedroom was in such a mess because we had the builders in (yet again – throughout the whole of my adult life it's been spirits and builders, I'm telling you), and Fiona was sitting on the bed with me on a tiny little stool at her feet, sort of staring up at her. Fiona had very few airs and graces which was lucky at a time like that.

'Do you know what?' I told her, 'I'm seeing a big problem with a sports star for the Princess.'

'What do you mean?' she asked, guardedly. (She knew what it meant, of course. Far more than I did. The Princess confided in her.)

I said, 'A photograph will be taken of the Princess of Wales and a sports star hiding behind her.'

As with so many of the things I spoke about with the Princess, I only found out exactly what this meant by reading the newspapers; I'd never get confirmation directly from the Princess; another difference between her and a usual client. It would either be from Carol or, latterly, Fiona, or from the tabloids. Sure enough, a very short time later there was a photograph of the Princess leaving a gym – and lurking behind her in the shadows was Will Carling.

I was never in any doubt, though, that the Princess consulted a lot of people like me. I'd say that if you were a good astrologer, a good medium, any kind of 'alternative' therapist ('crackpot', even) then the Princess of Wales found you. Because this was at a stage of her life when she was searching. She was looking for answers, for love, for advice and guidance. She was going through astrologers and mediums the same way she was going through men. And I don't mean that nastily. I just mean that in the period following her separation from Charles she went into overdrive. Searching, searching, desperate for advice. I think she didn't want to take responsibility for the massive changes she was going to inflict on the monarchy, so she hunted for people like me to try and see the future for her. Believe me, I'm under no illusions as to the part I played in the Princess's life. I know that she also saw Rita Rogers towards the end of her life. Dodi introduced her to Rita as far as I'm aware. Plus she saw an astrologer called Debbie Franks, and I know that, because on the odd occasion she'd call me Debbie by mistake and say, 'Oh, I'm so sorry, I call you Debbie and I call Debbie Sally.'

There were others, too. What I'm saying is, I don't want you to go away thinking, Sally Morgan's giving it the big one about how she spoke to the Princess of Wales every day. I was a small part of her life. We weren't 'best friends'; we'd talk on the phone at weird times, but then that was her way. The only time that ever got to be a real problem was when she rang me on Boxing Day, 1993.

*

It was a normal family Boxing Day. The girls. Mum and dad. Things between me and my parents still weren't right but I suppose you could say there was an uneasy truce. There was still a relationship of sorts. We no longer lived next door to them, of course, we were just getting settled, and though Jemma had never moved back in with us, neither did she live with mum and dad anymore. She had left home to start her own life, and as far as I was concerned she saw as much of me as she did of mum and dad, so all in all, it was about as good as it was going to get. Certainly, things were better at our house than they were at Sandringham, from where the Princess called me that morning.

She was on the phone for three hours. She must have asked me a hundred times if she was interfering with my family life and I guess I would have told her no, just to be polite, but come on, three hours on Boxing Day. Perhaps I would have been annoyed if she hadn't been in such obvious distress.

Wild horses won't drag out of me what was discussed during those three hours. What I can say is that she was concerned for her safety. She told me she thought her life was in danger and that she was going to leave the country for good.

She left Sandringham that day. The two boys remained with the rest of the family and Diana flew out.

If the Princess had perhaps hoped for a reconciliation with Charles then her hopes were finally, irrevocably shattered. No amount of clingy dresses could help her by then.

Twenty-Nine

I'm often asked, 'Why don't you use your gift on your-self?' To be honest, there's no easy answer. Why wasn't I able to see what happened to Fern? What's the point of knowing where some stranger's left her car keys if I can't see something happening to my little girl?

Sometimes I'm not sure if it's because I can't, or because I won't. Even after all these years I'm constantly amazed, frustrated and confused by what I can do. But I need to provide an answer to that question. What I usually say is that I don't want to use it for personal gain. I did check out Fern and Rebecca's husbands (both nice lads, of course), but that's as much as I've ever done. John's always on at me to have a go at predicting the lottery results but I don't. I just get this feeling it wouldn't work if I tried anyway.

I think sometimes it harks back to my childhood wish to go into nursing, and to that time in hospital with Fern. It's all interlinked and I'm still trying to make sense of it all; still wondering if I'll end this book having done so. Doubt it, somehow.

One theory I'd like to embrace is that I can only use my ability to help other people. I'm not a performing seal, though. So if I'm out socially, I never open – as in, I'm not open for business, and I'm not 'open'.

Ever since that fateful day at the Wimpy I've been really good at controlling what I do, so even though I do tend to see the odd spirit hanging round (and believe me, they crop up in the weirdest places: the supermarket, for example), I don't generally walk around seeing spirits in everyday life. What I'm saying is, I'm not a psychic sponge. It's a bit like, if you're a comedian and you're out for a drink with some friends you won't be telling jokes all night. Work is work.

Still, there is the odd occasion. I remember being at a dinner function once, and some of the other people around the table had been throwing the booze back and started clowning around. Okay, they were being bloody rude. If you've ever seen me on tour or on telly you'll know I like a laugh, yes? But I won't put up with anyone trying to make a monkey out of me. Which was exactly what was happening then.

I should have controlled it. By then I was a professional psychic. I was psychic to the Princess of Wales, for God's sake. I should have known better. What I did wasn't necessarily right, and I've never done anything like it since because I really do believe you shouldn't abuse your gift.

But maybe that's not strictly true because that night when a couple of the other guests were having a pop after too much pop, I started freaking them out.

I told one of the guys he needed to be careful moving slabs about in his garden and that shut the bugger up, because he was due to begin laying a patio the next day. One woman basically said she thought I was a liar (and if there's one thing that gets my goat, it's that); well,

I told her a few things. Maybe I went a bit too far, telling her something very private. She knew I wasn't lying after that. I turned my attention to another woman who had been lapping up all the mickey-taking when it was directed at me.

'And we both know what I could say to you,' I told her, and she burst into tears on the spot and ran to the toilet. I won't say, of course. But again, she knew I wasn't lying.

There was another occasion when I did a similar thing. I'd been doing a few charity events for the same group. Platform events, similar to the one I did at Kingston University. I must have helped raise tens of thousands of pounds for this particular charity, so I wasn't too impressed when one of the organizers started ripping into me after the event. You know what he did? He called me a fake. Silly sod's just seen me do this event, getting hit after hit among people he knows, so they're not 'plants' (the idea that psychics have a secret stash of Oscar-worthy actors and actresses to use as plants in the audience, by the way? That always gives me a chuckle), and here he is calling me a fake.

A couple of the other organizers were there, too, and I could see them shifting uncomfortably. Beside me I felt John bristle.

'Oh, I'm no fake,' I assured him, wearing my best polite smile.

'Go on, then,' he pressed. 'Why don't you tell me something about me that nobody else here knows?'

Like I say, silly sod. He'd just opened me up. Tell

you what, I see and hear some sights in my job, but what I then saw about him . . . it made me wince.

'You don't want me to do that,' I smiled.

'Come on. You can't do it, can you?'

'You sure you want me to?' I said, giving him every chance to get off the hook. 'It might embarrass you.'

'It won't embarrass me.'

'Really? So this afternoon when you were in the doctor's surgery and he had two fingers up your arse, giving you an anal examination, you're not embarrassed by that?'

The smile slid off his face. His colour rose.

'And you can't make up your mind whether or not to have the operation on your haemorrhoids,' I continued.

His mouth was opening and closing as he tried to get some words out, slowly turning redder and redder. A rather satisfying shade of red, if I do say so myself.

'Well, I think you'd better have the operation, don't you?' I added. 'Either that or you're going to have to keep on wearing the sanitary towels.'

'All right, all right,' he said, 'you're genuine. Stop. You're genuine.'

It makes a funny story, I suppose, which is why I'm telling it. But to be honest I'm not proud of using my talent in that way and my gut feeling is that I really shouldn't – I should use it to help people. So if I encounter disbelief then the best thing to do is laugh it off.

Those group meetings can be minefields anyway. There was one I did in South-West London for a group of vintage car buffs, all blokes of course. Middle-aged, middle class, a good bunch of blokes, but blokes nonetheless.

From the minute I got there I thought, 'Uh-oh, tough gig.' Because blokes, you know what they're like. If I do a reading for a man at a group reading or, these days, on tour, I don't need to be psychic to know how he'll sit. Arms folded. Bemused smile. Chin jutting out. Look on his face saying, 'Impress me if you can.' So you can imagine. A whole room full of them – I was looking at a sea of folded arms.

The best approach, I decided, was not to take myself too seriously. 'Bloody hell,' I told them, 'a bunch of car enthusiasts. Who decided it was a good idea to have an evening with a medium?'

Laughs accompanied a chap in the middle of the room as he raised his hand.

'Well don't you worry, love,' I told him. 'I can't fix your car but I'm a good medium. They'll all want my number off you after tonight, you mark my words.'

Yeah, right, said the folded arms, the jutting chins, the looks saying, 'Impress me if you can.'

But I did all right. I won them over. Like I say, I didn't take myself too seriously so I didn't leave myself open to ridicule and it was going well, nice and light-hearted, an entertaining evening.

Right up until the last bloke.

'And you needn't think you're getting away with it,' I said, pointing at him. He was sitting right in the middle. Sometimes I wonder if the spirit world does things like that deliberately. Come to think of it, I'm *sure* it does things like that deliberately. In response, he seemed to shrink into his seat, not a bloke who relished the limelight.

He was a popular chap, that much was clear from the way his mates were hooting with laughter, but there was something a bit shy about him, too.

'Don't you worry,' I told him, 'you've got nothing to worry ab . . .'

Oh but he did, I almost instantly realized as it hit me like a slap in the face, all the good fun of the evening suddenly draining away, becoming suddenly very serious.

The men in the room shifted a little, sensing the sudden change in atmosphere as I digested what I'd seen; then, carefully – very carefully – I said, 'Can I be honest with you, love? I think maybe you should see me later, cos I'm not sure you'll want everyone to hear this – it's a bit personal, darling.'

'It's okay,' he said, 'I've got nothing to hide.'

I could see others there were concerned for him. Nobody wants to hear something grim about a friend: 'Leave it, mate. See her in private, eh?'

'Nah,' he insisted, 'I'm big and ugly enough to take it. We've all come for a reading. I'm not having anyone say I bottled it.'

A laugh that floated nervously around the room.

'All right,' I said. 'You're adopted, aren't you?'

I could see a general look of confusion pass among the men; those that knew him well obviously thinking I'd got it wrong.

But he nodded. 'Yeah,' he agreed, 'I was adopted.'

At times like that, clients, and especially blokes, look at you differently. What they're expecting I'm not sure. But you come out with something like that – something you could never have known without access to all kinds of personal records – and they sit up and take notice.

'I'm going to tell you something you don't know,' I said. His eyebrows shot up. An expectant silence settled on the room. 'Would that be okay?'

He nodded. It was as though his friends were willing the news to be good.

'You have a twin brother.'

Now he was shaking his head. I was wrong, he was telling himself. The adopted thing? Just a fluke. A lucky guess, right? But he didn't have a brother . . .

'But your parents didn't tell you you were adopted until you were 15, did they?' I said.

He nodded agreement, stared hard. An intake of breath in the room. A collective 'how did she know that?'

(I wish I knew, guys, I wish I knew.)

'And they didn't want to drop that on you at the same time, but I'm telling you – you have a twin brother. I can see him. Spirit world is showing him to me.'

The brother was living in Hong Kong, where, I thought, he served in one of the forces. He wore a uniform, I knew that much.

And this guy believed me. There comes a time when you can't ignore the evidence in front of your eyes – even the biggest sceptic. If I could tell this guy he was adopted and that his parents revealed that fact to him when he was 15, then he had to put some faith in me. And sure enough, he began asking questions. Now he'd discovered he had a brother he wanted to know whether that meant he had to find him.

Well, no, I explained. But the spirit world had wanted to show this man his brother. Was it a coincidence that this guy was left until last in a room full of about 20 to 30 blokes and that he was sitting right in the middle? I don't know, but what I told him that night was that the spirit world was giving him this information for a reason – and I thought it was because his brother was trying to find him.

Well, that was that for the night. I left wondering if I'd hear anything else about it.

I did, luckily. He rang a few days later to tell me that he'd been quizzing his adoptive mother about his mysterious twin brother and she'd confirmed it. Now he was sifting through the paperwork for clues as to his sibling's whereabouts.

Some days later the phone rang again.

He'd found his brother, he told me. It was funny as it turned out: his brother's adoptive parents had revealed to him that he had a sibling and he'd been in the process of trying to track him down. He lived in Hong Kong, where he worked as a policeman.

Thirty

It was during a reading with Fiona that I predicted the death of the Princess. As with so many predictions I didn't realize its significance at the time. I misread it, I suppose. And why that happens I don't really know for sure – why so much of what the spirit world gives me should be so oblique, I mean.

The way I've always thought of the spirit plane is as a place that co-exists with our own but is not bound by our constraints of time or place. The notion of time, after all, is something we've developed on the earth plane. It's a unit of measurement. But spirits don't have that. They simply *are*. I imagine them viewing our plane with bemusement, wondering how they ever managed to cope with being so restrained by space, physicality, ageing. It must be like sprouting wings and learning how to fly.

What I'm often asked is how are you able to see the future? Why does talking to spirits allow you to see ahead? The way I see it, that's all because of this difference between our two planes. I describe it in terms of a train, racing along a track. On the earth plane we're passengers on that train. We know where we've been but we can only see a short way ahead – not far enough to see a tree on the track until it's too late.

Now imagine you're not bound by earthly laws. No

time or space. No body, nothing. You can rise way, way above and look down on the train, seeing what lies behind and what lies ahead. You can see that tree across the track way, way before anybody on the train will.

But here's where it can get frustrating. What if the spirit world doesn't have complete clarity of vision? Like me, it needs specs. And I know I'm in danger of exhausting this train comparison, but bear with me a moment longer. Perhaps spirit world can see *something* on the track, but it's not sure what. It might turn out to be a tree, but right now, it just looks like an obstruction. So often I explain to people that I can be wrong or I can misinterpret information (people's names, for example: Paula becomes Paul) but maybe it's not always me, it's a fault of the messenger? Perhaps spirit world can only see so much, only deliver so much of a message.

Yet again, I don't know for sure. You know how earlier I compared it to having a new video recorder? Well, I'm *still* working out how to programme it properly. All I know is, messages are rarely crystal clear. If they ever were, well, I'd be able to solve the world's problems, wouldn't I? I could sit down with world leaders and scientists, there'd be no such thing as sceptics (hurrah!) and I could have prevented the death of the Princess of Wales. Life's unfair, so they say. Perhaps so is the spirit world. Maybe life's unfair and so is death.

'Oh my God.'

I remember it as though it was yesterday.

It was August 1996. I'd been dealing with the Princess

for about four years then, taking calls from her regularly. There had been nothing quite as dramatic as the Boxing Day call but even so I'd witnessed much turbulence in her life. Since I first met her she'd officially separated from Charles, then announced her retirement from public life, both of which had been massive changes in her life. She was always very aware of her actions and what effect they could have on the British public and on the constitution. The night before that speech announcing her retirement, she called me to go over it, wanting to check the wording. Right down to individual words. She'd begun divorce proceedings. Stories about her private life were always in the papers but very few people knew the absolute truth (I refer you, though, to what I said before about the tabloids getting it right). Even so, the facts of what had happened that Boxing Day at Sandringham had never emerged. Neither had the details of at least one other affair she'd had – if that were ever to become public knowledge, it would stun the world. Me, I keep quiet about these things, because not only am I in the business of helping and not hurting people, but I do believe that divulging certain things could put me in danger – and that's all I'm going to say on the subject.

Anyway, back to the reading. I said, 'Oh my God.'

And Fiona said, 'Sally, what is it?'

'Oh my God,' I repeated. 'I really don't like what I'm seeing here.'

'What? What is it?'

'The Queen's going to die. She's going to die in a car accident.'

I could see a car. Blackness seeming to crowd in on it. I wasn't able to make out the car, just the darkness of its colour. And there was a body.

My hands flew to my mouth.

'Oh my God, Fiona,' I repeated. 'I can see them. They're pulling a body out of a car. Pulling her body out.'

It was dark, hazy, indistinct. But what I could see – I saw the body of a woman, most of it on the ground.

'. . . on concrete. It's a road. She's on a road . . .'

And her feet remained in the car. Whoever was pulling her out, they didn't pull her feet clear of the vehicle. Now I could feel a thumping against my own chest. In the vision I saw indistinct figures crowding around the prone body of the person – it was the Queen; somehow, I knew it to be the Queen – and I felt this thumping against my chest. They were trying to resuscitate her. She was lying on the road. The Queen was lying on the road somewhere dark, dying on the road as they tried to save her.

'It's very dark,' I said to Fiona. 'I feel like I'm in a tunnel and, oh my goodness me, the next week the Queen Mother dies.'

Fiona was staring at me. 'What? The Queen dies and the Queen Mother dies?'

'Yes,' I insisted. 'It's just a week later. I can see her funeral. First the Queen, then the Queen Mother.'

The vision ended, the reading came to a close. Fiona took the tape away to Kensington Palace and I suppose the Princess must have listened to it.

What happened to the tape then, I don't know. A year later, in August 1997, that tape would come back into my life, but for the time being I virtually forgot all about it; forgot all about the reading where I believed I'd witnessed the death of the Queen.

And Kensington Palace forgot about me. I never heard from the Princess of Wales again. I was to speak to Fiona one final time a year later, but I didn't have any other contact with her, either. Truth be told, I wasn't surprised.

Before this event, though, Diana had become close to Mohammed Al Fayed; she used to ask me about him.

'Why do you want to know?' I asked, one day.

'I've become very close to him.'

Shortly after that, of course, she met Dodi. It was one night as she was leaving Harrods with Mohammed Al Fayed that they passed one another on the escalators. Diana turned and said to Mohammed, 'Who's that?'

'That's my son.'

'Can I say hello?'

He called Dodi back down. History was being written.

One of the things she used to laugh about was that she was the new Jackie Onassis, and I think she very much wanted that older, almost father-figure man in her life. For that reason I don't think Dodi was the one for her. I'm positive they wouldn't have married. But it was around the time she was friendly with his father that she began to talk about being followed; about being watched. I must say, I never actually saw that. The vision I had where I saw the Queen being pulled from a car was really the one and only dark message I was ever given. But she was convinced that there were shadowy forces keeping an eye on her, and, well, I believe her. I didn't think about it too much, to be honest, but it's one of the reasons I still keep my mouth shut about certain things I know. I'm not scared, but I'm not stupid either.

What I can say about my time dealing with the Princess is that I saw her grow, and she definitely turned a corner when it came to her relationship with the Prince of Wales. In 1992 when I first met her, she clung onto the fairytale notion of kings and queens, princes and princesses. When it came to Prince Charles she had this idea that he might suddenly change his mind. She still hoped that he would love her the way she wanted to be loved, which was tactile, demonstrative. She couldn't understand that, well, to put it bluntly that's not his style, is it? He's just not that kind of man.

In a way, she was really quite childish about it. One of the reasons she clung to me and others like me was because she was desperate for guidance. The poor woman just needed help coming to terms with the position she suddenly found herself in. There's this popular image of her as being a bit soft-headed for believing in people like me: quacks. But it's not soft-headed to want help. Most people can rely on friends and family. What do you do when your family is the Royal Family and your father's an earl? When you're the most photographed woman in the world?

I'm not saying I was responsible for the change in her, no way. All I did was my best to help her understand that she had to change; that there was no point clinging to the past. With or without me, she would have awoken one morning and realized she was a new person. She was a bright, attractive, single woman. Her priorities lay with that and with her children.

Most importantly, she understood that, in her own way, she wielded an awful lot of power. The Princess of Wales in 1992 was intimidated by her in-laws. Not by 1996. She began playing games with them; goading them, you might even say.

'I can be me,' she used to say on the phone. 'I can be okay.'

Our chats were a form of counselling for her, that much I know. How much she got from me compared to the other people she spoke to, I'm really not sure, but I do know that she got compassion and understanding. I think she liked me. I like to believe she warmed to me. In the months after August 1996, the last time I had contact with her, it was wonderful to open the papers and see her so happy, so beautiful and so fulfilled. She'd gone from drowning to swimming. She thought they'd taken her life away but by sheer force of will, she'd won it back.

It's one of the reasons that what happened to her was so very, very tragic. She'd only just got her life back – then had it taken away from her.

Thirty-One

Meanwhile, I heard the Princess was telling people about me. I got wind of rumours that she'd been chatting about me in such-a-such a Royal box, and I suppose it's the same as with hairdressers, designers and chefs. If you want to go to a psychic you might as well go to one recommended by the Princess of Wales. So now I had wealthy and famous clients, and I'd often be whisked away to some amazing places simply to give readings. I was booked up all the time and doing very well. No doubt about it, professionally, I was achieving everything I'd ever wanted and more: I was using my gift to help people.

One of my clients worked in a very close capacity with Robert De Niro. Let's call her Laura. She was based in London but would go all over the world with him, accompanying him from film to film. Doing this job brought her into contact with the Hollywood crème de la crème so she became friendly with a number of big stars. Often, if they were working in or visiting London they might opt to stay with her, in more homely surroundings than a hotel, and free from the prying eyes of the paparazzi.

One Sunday morning, I happened to be at Laura's for a cup of coffee. Oh yes, and guess where she lived? That's right: Fulham. All roads lead to Fulham in my life story. I swear to God I could emigrate and something would pull me back there.

While I was there Laura asked me if I'd do a reading for someone called Uma. First thing to say is, I'm not the biggest film buff in the world, and this was mid-1997, before *Kill Bill* came out, and I didn't really have much of an idea who Uma Thurman was. She was in town overnight filming scenes for a new film, *The Avengers*, which, sadly for her and all concerned, is notable mainly for the fact that it was a massive flop.

Standing in Laura's kitchen I heard movement on the stairs and looked round to see a striking lady descending the steps, dressed in a bathrobe. (That, by the way, is how you dress when you're a famous person. Don't ask me why, but if you catch a celebrity at home or in their hotel room, chances are they'll be wearing a robe.)

'Oh, hello,' I said to her, cheery as ever, 'you must be Uma. Where are we doing your reading then, darling?'

Just then, striking lady number two appeared on the stairs behind lady number one, also in a bathrobe.

Both women burst out laughing. Striking lady number one pointed up the stairs behind her. '*This* is Uma,' she told me.

Turned out she was the assistant. I must've made her day. But Uma. My goodness, we are talking one seriously tall woman here. There was something about her that reminded me of Fern, too. Something facially. They're both blonde, and they have the same nose. As we sat down to do her reading, I found myself warming to her a great deal.

My reading threw up lots of private and personal things in Uma's life that I am not prepared to disclose. But what I will say is that I was able to tell her some exciting things about her career. I knew that it was going to take off, but not just at that moment. Now we know why, of course: she was in *Batman and Robin*, which flopped, and then *The Avengers*. But I told her I saw things going supernova soon, which turned out be the *Kill Bill* films she made with Quentin Tarantino.

If I'm honest, it wasn't one of my best readings. I've spoken before about the bond that is created between me and my sitter. The more receptive a person is, the more open I am.

I didn't see her again, and even if I had I wouldn't be talking about her in my book. This is because what almost everybody in this book has in common is firstly that I don't see them anymore, and secondly, that any secrets stay safe with me.

Which is why I can tell you about Robert De Niro, because despite some online PR to the contrary, I have never read for him. Nor, in fact, have I ever even met him, so let's put the record straight here.

In fact, it was *Mrs* Robert De Niro I had as a client.

She's Grace Hightower. This, again, was in 1997. They were married then; they nearly divorced some years later and as far as I know it was a bit on-off, but they're back together now.

I first met her at Laura's house. It was a bright summer's afternoon. When I arrived at her home, nobody was in, so I sat on a wall to wait, looking around at Fulham, at what had once been my home.

Again it's so weird, the way everything seems to lead back there. So bizarre. Fulham was where I grew up, where I met my husband, where I first saw spirits and was introduced to my gift. Later, the business was based there. And looking around, waiting for Laura and Grace, goodness, what a strange feeling. It was like these two worlds of mine, colliding in slow motion: my old Fulham life and my new life as a professional psychic about to meet Mrs Robert De bloomin' Niro, if you please. What would I have thought, if I'd been a little girl walking on the other side of the street? What would I have thought of the lady sitting on the wall?

Over there, I could see, there used to be a wet fish shop owned by a woman called Polly that Nanny Gladys absolutely loved. Polly used to wear a beret and I remember my mum stopping to talk to her with me standing beside her absolutely fascinated because she only had two or three teeth. Her whole mouth – just a couple of pegs in there.

Funny, I didn't feel at all out of place. It felt like being at home.

And then a Mercedes pulled up and Laura and Grace Hightower were piling out, weighed down by shopping bags, having spent an obscene amount of money in designer stores. I mean a lot of money. I have never seen so many shopping bags as appeared out of that car. This,

I thought, seeing all the shopping carted inside the house, is how the other half lives.

The other half being Grace Hightower, a lovely, tall black woman. Absolutely gorgeous, and really bubbly with it, too. Very outgoing, full of apologies that they'd kept me waiting, little knowing that I'd spent the time in a pleasant reverie.

'This is Grace, is it?' I said to Laura, as bag after bag came cascading out of the Mercedes.

'Yeah,' said Laura, whispering back. 'How did you guess?'

Inside the house I gave Grace a reading and it blew her away. As usual, I'm not going into the nitty gritty, but Grace was receptive and we created that bond that makes for a good reading. Put it this way, I knew I'd be hearing from her again, and sure enough I was doing phone readings for her very shortly afterwards.

And after that? Well, I was invited to Paris with her, where the De Niros had taken over an entire floor of one of the city's top hotels. I knew the hotel, funnily enough, having been a guest of an industrialist not long ago, but even so, being a guest of the De Niros was something else. I remember being picked up from the airport in a limo and being treated like the Queen. Travelling to the hotel, the prospect of spending four days with the couple seemed very exciting. As I've said, I'm not exactly Mrs Starstruck, but still, I thought, settling back into the comfort of the limo, I could seriously get used to this . . .

To be honest, though, it was a bit on the boring side. Nothing to do with Grace, who's an absolute diamond.

It was all that waiting around, and I missed John and the girls terribly.

For a start, I was there because Grace wanted me there. So that meant . . . well, there's no nice way of saying it, I was at her beck and call. You read about movie stars complaining how being on set is really, really boring and you think, 'Boring? Try doing a proper job if you think that's boring.' But the truth is, it *is* boring. Not because of the lack of things to do necessarily, but because you're constantly waiting to be called, so you can't get on with anything. I'm one of those people who like to be on time, and I like to be doing something. So to sit around doing nothing, and not really able to start doing anything in case you're summoned, is torture for someone like me. I'm not saying I won't consider the job if I ever get called upon to stand in for Julia Roberts, but I think I've got a better idea of what they're going on about now.

Plus it was almost as if there were two camps in one: the Grace camp and the Robert camp. That meant that I didn't get to meet him at all. There was one morning when we were supposed to meet but he went off in a helicopter to look at locations for an upcoming film project. I remember shortly afterwards going to Grace's suite where she was wearing a bathrobe (naturally) and worrying that he'd left his hat behind. She's a lovely lady, Grace. What people forget is how hard it can be for women to come into a set-up like that. Someone like De Niro – in fact any powerful, successful man – has a huge entourage. And many of these people will have been working with him since the year dot, for film after film after film. So anybody coming into that, who's not only coming into it fresh, but in a 'high-ranking' position, if you like – and it doesn't get much more high-ranking than 'wife' – gets treated like an outsider; with distrust and suspicion. For a woman in that position – and Grace was expecting, so probably felt even more vulnerable – having someone like me around had to be a comfort, and I think I was well aware of that being my function during those four days. I was just there to be in Grace's corner, really. Her main concern during that period was being 'let in'. It reminded me in many ways of the situation with the Princess of Wales.

Except with one crucial difference, of course. Things seem to have worked out for those two. Somehow they found some space in that mad bubble for each other. More power to them I suppose. Grace and I have just about kept in touch since that time and we're due to get together again soon. I have a feeling that the Grace Hightower I'd meet now would be considerably more settled and secure than the one I met then.

Another strong couple I met around the same time was the Garfunkels, when Kim, Art's wife, became a client of mine. She's still a client, so I won't say much about her, except that she's an incredibly courageous woman and has struggled bravely with cancer. Again, I don't want to go into details, but she's a great supporter of cancer charities and we've become very close. I like to think that I've been able to help her through some very, very tough times and in return she's been . . . okay, at the risk of sounding a bit cheesy, a real inspiration to me.

When you know and work with someone who's dealing with cancer, you can't help but view your own problems in a different light. Someone who has cancer is staring down death every day. Kim's one of those very people. And through her I've met some extraordinary characters. Not only her husband, Art, who's an incredible bloke, very, very thoughtful and artistic, but other cancer sufferers and again, they're a very inspiring crowd. There in the Garfunkels' New York apartment – and these guys are almost like American royalty – you don't really expect to be moved in that way. I can't say I'm a tremendously 'lucky' person – I've had some luck to turn your hair grey, but I've been lucky to meet so many incredible people: the people who came to see me at home, those I travelled to see, the De Niros, the Garfunkels, the Princess of Wales, for goodness sake.

And then, on August 31, 1997, a prediction I barely even remembered came horribly true.

Thirty-Two

You and I won't live long enough to know the full story of what really happened to the Princess of Wales.

I always use the analogy of the two princes imprisoned in the Tower of London in 1483, their skeletons discovered in 1674. Debate still rages as to exactly what happened to them and that, I think, is how the death of the Princess of Wales will be considered in centuries to come. What began as a rumour in 1483 has, hundreds of years later, become something we think of as common knowledge; that the two princes in the tower were executed on the orders of their uncle, Richard III. I wonder what today's rumours will have become in 500 years' time. Still conjecture? Or will they have become fact?

What I do think is that the Princess was right: they were out to get her. Who are 'they'? I don't know, to be honest, I really don't. But I do believe there is a 'they', and that they are very, very powerful indeed. Initially, they just wanted to keep tabs on her. But she was a child who craved attention. She became too extreme and ended up paying with her life.

Like everybody else in the world, I can remember exactly what I was doing when I heard about her death. I was in bed. John had got up, I recall. It was very early, and the next thing I knew he was shouting for me from the bottom of the stairs, a note of, well, almost panic in his voice.

'What's going on?' I called back, groggily.

He was pounding up the stairs. 'You've got to get up,' he said, breathlessly, at the door of the bedroom. 'Princess Diana is dead.'

It's a dream, I thought. I'm still asleep and I'm dreaming.

Or it's one of John's jokes (but in very bad taste, John, very bad taste).

Or I misheard him.

Or someone's got it wrong.

My mind was slowly, sleepily processing these possibilities, untangling things in my head: the note of panic and worry in John's voice, the sound of the TV from downstairs from which I could clearly the words 'Princess of Wales'. It was louder than usual.

'You what?'

I sat up. The princess is dead? She can't be dead. I saw her in the papers yesterday. She can't be dead.

'I'm telling you,' he said, and he was already disappearing back downstairs to check on the news reports, me following not far behind.

Not a joke. I hadn't misheard him, and nobody had got it wrong. Or if they had then *everybody* had got it wrong, because on every channel it was the same. The same images of the Princess or red-hued footage of the tunnel.

'Diana, Princess of Wales, is dead.'

I hugged myself. Suddenly feeling very, very cold indeed.

is concerned is no, because I'm a psychic and we're the kind of people who are easy to discredit. I could put virtually anything about the Princess in a book and people could say I'm making it up, and that's fair enough, I suppose. So, no, I don't worry about the things I know about the Royal Family. Other clients, though, have forced me to take certain measures. Obviously, I'm not going to say who, but I see the wives of some very, very powerful men, some of whom have done vile things in their rise to power. Like it or not, I've seen many of these deeds during readings. The readings are recorded on tape, the women take the tapes home and, like a lot of clients, I suppose, their nearest and dearest get to listen to them – so you get situations where the husband knows that I know. Put it this way, I have written a letter which is deposited in a bank overseas. In the event of my death in mysterious circumstances this letter will be opened.

Mohammed Al Fayed knows more than he's ever let on. But some of the things he knows are so outlandish, nobody would believe him; the things he said would be discredited as the ravings of a grieving father and friend of the Princess. It's my opinion that he would have very much liked the Princess of Wales as a daughter-in-law, but she wouldn't have married Dodi. She was very much enjoying his company, that's for sure, but as for marriage? No. Sorry, but the man she loved was the heart surgeon, Hasnat Khan. It's often written that he was the great love of her life, and even though the inquest revealed that *she* had apparently dumped *him*, this was absolutely true. I don't know the exact circumstances of the beginning of her association with the Fayeds – I hope for her sake there was more to it than thumbing her nose at the Palace – but I do sometimes wonder if getting involved with them was the worst thing she could have done.

Conspiracy theories around the death of the Princess took a while to surface, and to be honest, apart from an uneasy feeling about the whole thing, I don't think I'd really given the circumstances of her death much thought. I was still riding that wave of disbelief that seemed to settle on the country, on London in particular. You could feel it on the streets and in the shops. There was a sense of people being subdued, shocked. Everywhere you looked was a reminder. Every television news report was full of it: the Princess of Wales was dead.

Then, four days after the funeral, I had a phone call.

'Hello, Sally.' It was Fiona.

'Oh, hello,' I said, surprised because she really was the very last person I expected to hear from.

As usual, I started rabbiting on. 'Fancy thinking of me. You must have a lot on your plate; it's only been four days since the funeral.'

'Yes.' She sounded exhausted, washed out.

'It must be so hard for you, darling. You haven't been able to grieve, have you? You're watching the whole country grieve for the person that you should be grieving for.'

'Yes.'

'I'm so sorry, sweetheart. What can I do? Tell me what I can do to help.'

She cleared her throat as if to announce a change in

tone. 'I had to ring you,' she said. 'There are people who want to see you. They've listened to the tape.'

'What tape?' I said, mind racing, still not quite putting two and two together.

'The tape, Sally, the tape.'

'What tape?'

'The tape. Don't you remember, Sally? You predicted her death.'

And it clicked.

You may be thinking, what a dozy old thing, forgetting a tape like that, but you have to remember that I've been psychic all my life, a working psychic since 1990 and I've done *thousands* of readings in that time. I don't remember every single one; not even the really eventful ones. I don't have a list of predictions that I can tick off as they happen. What tends to happen is I get moments like that one, where I'm reminded of something I've predicted.

The tunnel, the darkness, a body dragged out of a car. The *thump thump* in my chest.

I caught my breath.

'You predicted her death,' Fiona was saying.

'Did I?'

'Yes.'

'I said the Queen, Fiona,' I managed, finding the words difficult to form.

'Yes, and after that Diana said she wanted to be known as the queen of people's hearts. Then you said that a week later the Queen Mother would die.'

'Well the Queen Mother's still alive.'

'You saw her funeral, didn't you?'

'Yes.'

'Sally, the Palace has certain funeral plans. State funerals, you know? The funeral given to Diana was the Queen Mother's funeral. That's why you saw the Queen Mother's funeral.'

I felt goosebumps rise on my forearms, conscious suddenly that she was right. Fiona was right: I'd seen the death of the Princess of Wales, right before my eyes and yet . . . nobody had guessed. It hit me then that Fiona would have taken the tape and played it to the Princess. Oh, God: a year before it happened she heard a prediction of her own death. Was that why she broke contact? Somehow me talking about death, so different to our usual conversations about her love life – somehow it had all got a bit too serious for her.

Fiona was still talking, telling me how I'd spoken of the *thump thump* to the chest; how the Princess had been pronounced dead of a coronary.

'You said they would thump her chest at the roadside and they did. You said it would happen in a tunnel and it did.'

'Right.' I was still trying to take it all in. Still trying to banish the image of the Princess listening to the tape – hearing me describe her death. Unwittingly, it seemed, I'd broken one of my golden rules.

'They've listened to the tape.'

They?

'Who?' I said.

'Some very, very important people,' she said, 'and they want to meet you.'

'Right,' I said, slowly. 'Okay.'

'There will be three of them.'

'Right. When . . . when did they listen to the tape?'

'On the train.'

'Right.'

'How do you think she died, Sally?'

'I don't understand what you — a car crash. It was an accident, wasn't it?'

'Do you think? Are you sure it was an accident?'

'Are you asking me as a person or as a psychic?'

'Either. Both.'

'I think it was an accident,' I said.

There was a long pause. 'Right. Okay.' Then, 'Sally, can I ask you to promise me you'll always say it was an accident.'

'Okay,' I said.

Why, though? Why did she want me to say that? To preserve the status quo? Or for my own protection? Because at that point, remember, it was all so fresh, everybody was still in shock. I honestly wasn't thinking about any conspiracy. Along with everybody else I thought it was an accident. The spirit world hadn't shown me anything to the contrary — and still hasn't. It was easy for me to agree to Fiona's request. But in the years since I've had time to dwell on the things said to me by the Princess. I was reminded of that old saying, 'It's not paranoia if they're really out to get you.' I recalled what the Princess used to say about being watched. Fear that used to trickle down the phone to me. One night, very late, she'd told me about a member of her security who had 'said something to me about vehicles and a car'. A comment that at the time had passed me by, but that now leapt out at me.

I agreed to Fiona's request never to say it was anything but an accident (whether I've since abided by it is another matter), but it was from that moment on that I began to form my own suspicions about the death of the Princess.

Fiona continued. She was telling me about the three people who wanted to see me. How I would get a phone call and be taken to London. We'd change vehicles then go off to a discreet location. Would this be okay with me?

Yes, I replied, though, to be honest, the whole thing was starting to give me the heebie-jeebies.

'And remember,' she said, 'whatever they ask you, whatever they say, you tell them you think it was an accident.'

(For my own protection, then. She made me promise for my own protection.)

If I were ever to compile a list of Clandestine Meetings I'm Secretly Pleased Never Actually Took Place, then this one would be at the top of it, because it never did.

There never was a call. There was no swapping cars and no three high-level people. And I'm not just saying that because men in black suits and sunglasses shoved bamboo under my fingernails. It honestly never happened.

'They' never called.

I've since had a lot of time to think about the meeting that never happened. Perhaps I should have been a little bit more inquisitive that day on the phone. But there was something about Fiona's tone that stopped me asking any further questions. Since then I've been over and over it. Who were the three people? 'The train' – what was all that about?

Well, the Princess's coffin went by car from Westminster Abbey to Althorp. Everyone else went by train. Was it then? I've gone over this in my head for more than a decade. If it was then, why did Fiona have the tape with her on that day? Where would they have played it? Why would they want to listen to a psychic's tape after an event like that? It doesn't make any sense.

But, of course, nothing surrounding the Princess' death makes much sense.

There's a little postscript to this story. Years later, Kim Garfunkel invited me to see Simon and Garfunkel play at Hyde Park, and John and I were milling around backstage (as you do, la-di-da) when we bumped into Koo Stark. She's a bit of a friend, and also knows Kim, and when she saw me she took me to one side. She told me that she'd been interviewed the previous day. I was going to get a call, she said, and would have to appear at the inquest.

'They asked me if I knew you and I had to say I did,' she said.

Another call that didn't come. And if I had to compile a list of Inquests I'm Glad I Didn't Attend, that one would have been at the top.

Thirty-Three

I have seen some frightening and distressing things thanks to my friends in the spirit world. As I've said, they know I can handle it; I believe that's one of the reasons I was chosen for the purpose, part of the complicated formula that somehow makes me able to do this job.

It doesn't make it any easier, though. It doesn't help when I'm being forced to see what I see.

There were four of them, dressed in the fashion of the day: sharp suits; narrow, black ties; Brylcreem in their hair, combed into smart side-partings. You might have taken them for respectable men, were it not for something about them: their language, for a start, but something else, too. They stood in an alleyway smoking, waiting, talking in low voices. Every other word was a profanity. Three of the men seemed to defer to the fourth. They stood plotting in a circle but it was this fourth man who was the leader, who was giving orders. From them all there seemed to emanate a darkness, but around this man the air was thicker, more malevolent. In the wet, dank alleyway, his voice was a low, evil murmur.

It was Reggie Kray.

The funny thing was, a moment earlier he'd seemed so nice. I was chatting to him and his brother Ronnie, both of them in spirit, and they were letting me know about the family. Their mother, Violet, was with them. If you've seen the film or read anything about the Krays you'll know that they worshipped their mother, so both of them were as pleased as punch to be with her in the spirit world, or, 'f-in' over the moon abaht it,' as Reggie said, before apologizing for his language.

The session was being filmed for a DVD documentary about them, so I was changing the odd word here and there, for the benefit of the audience. Even so, I felt like saying, 'Do you kiss your mother with that mouth?'

Even before filming had begun I'd blown a light bulb. This happens a lot with me actually, especially where film crews are concerned. They all have these lighting rigs, and it's a regular occurrence that a bulb will blow – it happened to me on *This Morning* as well but on that occasion, as happens most times, it was just the one bulb. Sitting down to contact the Krays, two had gone.

Perhaps it was because there were two of them? Who knows. Either way, filming had to be delayed while the lights were fixed. Then, when they were eventually operational and I began the reading, they seemed to dim as I felt the spirits of the two Krays arrive in the room, one either side of me.

Ronnie was the reserved one of the two, leaving most of the talking to Reggie, who seemed happy for me to pass on details of what he was up to in the spirit world. Nothing too hair-raising, I'm pleased to say – being dead has obviously mellowed them. Aside from being f-in' pleased about being with Violet, they were f-in' pleased their brother Charlie was with them, while Reggie was f-in' over the moon to see to his first wife, Frances. She had come to him just as he died, he told me. Hers was the first spirit he met in the other plane. He was looking forward to seeing his widow, Roberta, he added, but all in good time. You've got to be careful passing on a message like that one. Coming from Reggie Kray it can seem like a threat, but I'm fairly positive he meant it.

I must admit, it was all very homely and friendly and with the exception of the f-in' swearing, I could have been talking to any normal spirit . . .

Right up to the end, when Reggie told me about that night.

He wasn't just telling me about it, either, but showing it to me. Taking me into that alleyway, putting me behind his shoulder to hear the murmured plotting (though not the actual words), then into a nightclub. I don't know where exactly, but it was a West End nightclub. Now they had a fifth man, a prisoner. His hands and feet were bound with something that might have been a washing line. They were in a car now, driving, and I know they'd driven for about 40 minutes before they arrived at the spot where they got out of the car and lit up cigarettes, one of the men untying the prisoner and tossing him a spade pulled from the boot of the car.

The darkness crowded in on the scene, like watching an old, old silent film, where the edges of the frame seem hazy and fuzzy. So I couldn't see precisely where we were. But I somehow knew that we were in Essex.

In a graveyard.

I wanted to pull away from the scene, banish the

image, not knowing exactly what was going to happen, but horribly aware that this man – tall, middle-aged, a big bloke, whimpering, pleading for his life – was about to die.

Reggie toed the ground with one immaculate shoe, indicating the spot and the man began to dig. For a moment or so I was forced to watch, hearing the scrape of the shovel on the earth, seeing moonlight reflected off tears that ran freely down the dying man's face. Because that's what he was: a dying man. There was talking, but I wasn't allowed to hear it. The only sound was the slow, chop-dig of the spade, feet moving around on the soft earth.

He tried to stop. Several times he wanted to stop digging, but they made him continue. The image seemed to cut forward until the hole was sufficiently big enough for their purpose.

One of the men wanted to gag the prisoner. Reggie looked around as though to say, 'Who would hear?'

The man dropped to his knees, staring up at Reggie, saying something, wet eyes beseeching him, pleading for mercy. Reggie grinned. Then he kicked him into the hole.

He tried to stand. They kicked him back into the hole. One of them brandished the shovel to stop him trying again.

Then they began to fill in the hole.

The whole time Reggie screamed at him, his finger pointing, as though to make the dying man know exactly why he was being killed. And how agonizing it would be.

The last I saw of him as dirt rained down on him was his mouth, wide open and screaming.

They continued shovelling dirt on top of the hole until it formed a mound, which they stamped upon. The mound was still visible, but – I don't know – either it was in some out-of-the-way part of the graveyard or they had some kind of arrangement with a grave digger. They left it and went back to their car, returning to London.

All Reggie would tell me was that Ronnie hadn't been involved and that two of the guys involved in the killing were still alive. The wife of the man buried alive knew about the murder but she was paid off; she'd since built a new life for herself, remarrying and moving on.

I later discovered that on his deathbed in 2000 – two years before I did the reading – Reggie had admitted to a murder, one the police think was this man that I'll call Teddy Smith, though it's never been officially confirmed.

'I did a good job there,' Reggie told me, smiling.

Ugh.

I came out of the reading shaking, suppressing a cold shiver – the same way I felt when I thought about the Princess inadvertently hearing the tape of her own death.

Is it worth it? I wondered. Do I want all this? Do I really want to see this?

Because . . . well, it's bizarre. The picture I've formed of spirit world over the years is of a place unified and motivated by love. Which makes it sound like some kind of after-death equivalent of Woodstock. And maybe that's true. I hope it's true. It can't be the *whole* truth, though, can it?

Can it?

Is it possible that the Kray twins, one of whom I'd

seen screaming obscenities at a man buried alive on his orders, have been accepted by the spirit world with open arms? Is the spirit world really that . . . undiscerning.

And what of their victim? The man who died with earth forcing its way into his eyes, ears and mouth. Was there anyone on the spirit plane to greet him at his last dirt-filled breath? What happens to all that pain and torment?

As psychics, I think we're sometimes guilty of inventing easy answers to complex questions. Answers we hope the world will understand so the world will understand us. But what if there are no easy answers? What if we're not meant to comprehend what happens over there? We're just conduits for it. After all, you don't need to know how a TV works to watch *EastEnders*, do you?

What I'm sure of, though, is that there are no such things as limbos or lower planes. I've been involved with many crime cases – the stories will have to wait until another time, I'm afraid – and working on cases involving violent death I've become sure there are no secret levels of spirit world. I'm certain of this because as far as I'm concerned there is only one spirit world, and I've spoken to many, many people there, among them, murderers, victims, suicides. So if I was trying to make sense of it, I suppose I might say that somehow we all live as part of a pre-ordained plan while on the earth plane, so that when we pass over we're simply fulfilling a role in the grand scheme of things. Either our deeds on the earth plane are forgotten or just not really relevant because we were only fulfilling our destiny. To play out some kind of afterlife game of heaven and hell just wouldn't be fair if that were the case.

Maybe that's how it works.

Or maybe not.

After all, is it possible to comprehend a plan that includes the Holocaust, the Asian Tsunami in 2004 and the Chinese earthquake of May 2008?

A plan that includes September 11, 2001?

Thirty-Four

It was about two pm when the news came in. I was working, of course, seeing clients. I wonder how many I've seen in my office over the years? Thousands, certainly; all needing help of one kind or another, whether it's contacting a loved one or choosing a nanny for their child.

All of those problems I've helped to solve. Yet my own I could do nothing about. I have remained estranged from Jemma. She has kept in contact with Fern, Rebecca and Gina so at least I have known she is okay, and have followed her career in the police force with pride.

But I haven't seen her. I haven't spoken to her.

'It's like death but not,' I have found myself saying.

So I did what so many do. I blocked it out by working. I threw myself into my work. All the heartache, well, I used it. Whatever doesn't kill you and all that.

And so it was that I was working that day, coming out from my office with a client to find John talking about a plane that had hit the Twin Towers.

Like the morning that the Princess of Wales died, suddenly every TV channel had an image of the Twin Towers with black smoke pouring from them, a terrifying, chilling image.

'Big tall building like that,' said John, 'it was inevitable something like that would happen one day.'

'No,' I said, 'that isn't it. This is deliberate, you mark my words.'

Then the telephones began to ring. We had six phone lines in those days, just to cope with the business. And every single one of them began to sing out.

On the phones were clients from all over, from America in particular. One was Asian but he lived in Hong Kong; and used to ask me about the markets. At the time of the Twin Towers being hit he was on a flight to America and he called me from First Class. They were diverting his plane to Canada and wouldn't give him any information. He wanted to know what was going on but all his business lines were busy, his wife unavailable. He thought of me. Other clients wanted to know what was next. I had people who lived in Manhattan calling me in hysterics. High-ranking London types wanting to know if the City was next.

And next a journalist friend of mine called Claire – Claire Davey. She worked for *Eve* magazine at the time.

'Are you watching TV, Sally?'

'Oh my God, sweetheart, how awful is this?'

'You predicted it.'

Déjà vu, or what?

'Did I?'

Just as the second plane hit.

'Claire, let's talk later, all right?'

The rest of the day I fielded calls from worried clients. Then, during the evening, I got to talk to Claire, who reminded me about the prediction. I'd made it the previous year, she said. She had the tape of me describing a modern-looking city on an island – Manhattan Island – with lots of tall buildings, two of which were particularly imposing. Virtually identical, they stood next to one another. But I'd said that I could see them collapsing. I had said that two planes would be involved and that the two towers would fall, causing some kind of flooding in the underground tunnels.

It was only later that I read that the two tunnels beneath the Hudson River between New York and New Jersey had been completely flooded as a result.

At the time, of course, I hadn't given the prediction much thought – as with any other prediction, really. Nor had Claire. By then I had made a bit of a name for myself: it had become public knowledge that I'd been the Princess of Wales's psychic, I was often in magazines and I'd done a bit of TV work. But either way that particular prophecy hadn't made it – it was really only the fact that Claire kept the tape and remembered about it later that brought it to light.

After that conversation I began thinking about other occasions I might have foreseen the attack. I had an American client called Diane. She had come to me seeking advice about her career options but during the reading I'd warned her about a friend, Dan. She confirmed she had a friend called Dan.

'Somehow, I don't know how, but I'm being told that he'll be connected to a large disaster,' I told her. 'It will involve a plane crashing into a building in New York. The military will be involved and the disaster will have a huge impact on the United States.'

Well, I was right. He was indeed connected. His wife, Lauren, worked at the World Trade Center and was there on the day of the attack. She was one of the lucky ones.

That was a reading from 1992. Again, in 1998, I spoke to Diane's husband and I got something very similar.

It often makes me wonder, though. If somehow I had realized that it was 9/11 I was seeing, and somehow I had a hotline to President Bush, who believed every word that I said. Could I have prevented it with that prediction?

By having a vision of the Princess of Wales dying, could I have advised her never to drive in another tunnel? Because she trusted me would she have ordered Henri Paul not to go through the Pont de l'Alma tunnel that night? Could I have changed history?

In theory, yes. Which sort of makes a mockery of my previous suggestion that perhaps the path of our lives is pre-destined. Yet I can't change history, and never will. Even if someone gets a prediction and acts to change it, then I believe that action is built into the prediction. And for something as (seemingly) random as 9/11 or the death of the Princess of Wales, it's as though the messages passed on from the spirit world are deliberately oblique. Why? Who can say? I mean, why bother giving out messages at all if nobody can interpret them successfully? If the spirit world wanted people like me to be taken more seriously on the earth plane then why not give us specifics? Details?

One more question to add to the list of things I have yet to learn about, I guess.

*

After the attack, I went to America where I had a lot of clients needing help: many were women who had lost their husbands, and there were some incredibly traumatic readings during that period. One woman, I'll never ever forget it, she pulled out a watch which had dried blood on it. It was a lovely analogue watch, with a leather strap that had been cut when it had been removed from her husband's wrist.

She placed it on the table and I looked down at it.

'Your husband jumped, didn't he?' I told her. I saw it. It makes me go cold just to think of it now. I saw his body, and it was if it was completely intact, but only one half of it. It looked as though someone had taken a knife and cut him from top to toe and discarded one half. As he'd fallen from the building he'd banged against the structure and it had mutilated that half of his body. It was horrific, truly horrific.

As I say, most of the readings I had around that time were with wives wanting either to know about how their husbands had died or to take comfort that they were now doing well in the spirit world. Talking to them, what I learnt was that most of the deaths had at least been painless. Most of the casualties occurred when the towers collapsed and they literally knew nothing of it.

I spoke to one woman whose husband called her from underneath a table and she said, 'He was telling me how much he loved me and he said, "Can you hear that noise?"'

She said to him, 'I can't hear it, what noise?'

And the line went dead. Those were the last words he

said to her and she was so upset that she had been unable to hear the rumble that he heard. I saw nine people who lost loved ones in 9/11. Of those, two had died after jumping and at least parts of their bodies had been recovered. These two ladies had some personal effects, however meagre, because their husbands' bodies had been cleared before the towers came down. The other seven ladies, though, had nothing – nothing came out of that pile of rubble that was recognizably human. Not even an object. For those women, being able to receive messages from their husbands in spirit was a tremendous comfort.

For the next two or three years I spent several months a year in New York. I virtually had a practice there.

Meanwhile, back in the UK, word about me was spreading. I was doing a lot of work for magazines, a lot of it predictions or chatting to late celebrities such as Audrey Hepburn, Clark Gable, Vivien Leigh and Marilyn Monroe. I would be given questions to ask them, and be able to describe the rooms in which they were sitting.

And then, of course, there was the 'business' with Mel B. And things *really* took off.

What happened was that Mel B came to see me one day. This was early in 2001 and the Spice Girls were still together, though I suppose you might say this was at the tail end of their first phase as a band.

'Oh, hello, love,' I said as she came bustling in for her appointment. Under her arm she had several framed photographs. Most people bring photographs but I have to say they normally take them out of the frames. Scary Spice had just grabbed a load of them from the wall of her home and tossed them into her car before driving over. Not little pictures, either: they were huge.

There in a nutshell, in that one action, was all you needed to know about Mel B. She's nuts. Lovely and charming but chaotic and wonderfully nuts. I don't think she'd mind me saying that.

You know I'm not going to tell you what I said during the reading. But it went well. Suffice to say, I hope she's listened to the tape recently because every time I see her in the papers these days it seems another one of my predictions has come true.

Anyway, two days later there was a knock at my door. Normally John gets it, but sod's law he was out so I answered it myself.

Welcome to the world of the tabloid press.

There were two of them and I could see that one of them had a camera – the kind you see paparazzi wielding these days. The other, wearing a smart suit, spoke.

'Are you Sally Morgan?'

'Yes,' I said. Call me psychic, but I knew something was up!

'We'd like to talk to you about the Spice Girls.'

Uh oh, I thought.

'I don't understand,' I said, understanding perfectly well what he meant by talking about the Spice Girls – and it wasn't to ask about my favourite album.

'We hear you've seen the Spice Girls,' he said.

I was in the middle of a reading at the time. A well-known businessman. Let's just call him Frank.

'Well you've heard wrong,' I said, not really fibbing because, after all, I'd only actually seen Mel B, hadn't I?

'Well we know you've seen Mel B.'

'Well I think you're mistaken.'

'Look, Sal,' he said, and it was as if he was doing an impersonation of a gutter journalist. Calling me Sal. I ask you. 'I'm from *The People*. Let's cut the crap, shall we?'

And then he put his foot in my door. Not very original, but I suppose there's a reason they have a reputation for doing that. It's because it works. Next, the photographer started taking pictures of my house.

Click. Flash.

Just as my new friend the tabloid journalist was telling me, 'The story's being run Sunday whether you like it or not and we've already got the details of it.'

I was pushing the door by now, calling round it, 'Well what you coming round here for then?'

Click. Flash.

'Won't you even give us a . . .'

Frank told me later that he'd been diving for cover in my office when the camera flash started going, thinking for some reason that they were trying to take pictures of him. Bless. Fortunately for me, he either overheard that we were talking about Mel B, or simply came to the conclusion that he probably wasn't a newsworthy item for the *Sunday People* and came to my rescue.

I was really leaning into the door by then. 'No, I won't,' I called, just as he came to his senses, came out of the office, marched to the door and opened it wide.

The journalist removed his foot as the two of them had words, Frank telling them to clear off.

They left, me and Frank going back to the office, me filling him in on the story. How Mel B had come for a reading, and now . . .

'You don't know who Mel B is, do you, Frank?' I said.

He shook his head.

'The Spice Girls?'

Still no.

Even so, I had to excuse myself to make a call to Mel, telling her what had just happened.

'I didn't tell them anything. I've got a witness here, Mel, whatever they know didn't come from me, no way. But they say they're going to run it. Anything they've got, they didn't get from me.'

When she'd made the appointment the whole thing had been a huge secret arrangement. A client had asked if her friend 'Melanie' could come, and there had been all this talk about confidentiality. Obviously I'd puffed up and told them no way would I ever tell a soul. Which I never would. Next thing you know I've got half of Fleet Street at the door. And considering my clientele, this was not good for business.

There was a silence.

'Mel?' I prompted.

'Oh no,' she moaned at the other end of the line.

'What?'

'Oh no. I know what it is.'

'What?'

'When I left you, I put the tape in the car.'

In those days, I used to wrap the tape in a compliments slip and – ping – put an elastic band around it. Mel had opened the tape, discarded the compliments slip, then, the next day, her Range Rover had gone in for a service.

'Someone must have put two and two together and phoned the paper,' she concluded.

'Well as long as you know it didn't come from my camp,' I said.

It certainly didn't. But when I saw the piece in the paper, well, I had to wonder where the information *did* come from. There was stuff in the report that certainly wasn't on the tape. Hmm . . .

I learnt a bit of a lesson there. Stars do love their PR. And these days, I'm a bit more savvy about it. If a paper calls to ask if I've seen certain members of a certain very popular girl band, I know not to panic. I know that it's just the wheels of celebrity turning.

Don't get me wrong, no way am I saying that members of a very popular girl band leave my house, pick up the phone and talk to the tabloids. I don't believe any celebrity would do that. But their managers and agents? The people paid to make sure their client stays in the public eye? That's another story.

You know how they say you should never believe what you read in the papers? As I've mentioned before, in my experience you should believe more of it than they're given credit for. What you might want to take with a pinch of salt is exactly how that information got there.

For me, of course, that story was exposure. No managers or agents needed. No desire, even, to get into the public eye. It just sort of 'happened'. Slowly, through word of mouth and a series of fortuitous circumstances, I was making a name for myself not just as a psychic, but as a *celebrity* psychic, and before you know it, it's like chucking-out time at the Ivy on my drive. I'm not kidding you, I had soap stars, actors, actresses, sports stars, singers, bands, presenters and models. I've contacted dead people to help actors research, I've looked at sports injuries, I've seen sex scandals to turn your hair grey. And drugs: I've seen more habits than a laundry at a convent. On the one hand, yes, it's very flattering that all these successful people want to see me; that they know I'm good and that I'm the real deal; on the other, it means I have to deal with an awful lot of traumatic fall-out. Because, you know, for every bit of gossip and tittle-tattle there's heartache and tears. The actress raped by a fellow actor (you'd have heard of them both): that's not pretty. That's not easy to deal with. I'm pleased to say I was able to help. Another actor, drugged, only to wake up to find himself being filmed having sex – with another man. Nasty. It didn't make the papers, that one, but you should have seen the state of the poor lad. At times like that you realize – it's worth thinking about the human cost behind the headlines.

Thirty-Five

When you reach something approaching the top of your field, suddenly everyone wants a pop at you. In my case, of course, I attract the sceptics. I get people wanting to 'test' me all the time. I do this stuff every day: for over a decade I saw around six clients a day and do you know that they were doing? They were testing me. I've worked in New York and Australia, seeing clients, being tested. I've been on television, and guess what happens when you go on telly? They want to test you. Newspapers send reporters to write features, and they test you.

I am so sick of being tested, you wouldn't believe. I'm constantly being asked to explain exactly what I do, as though I understand it all perfectly myself. Try asking a runner to explain exactly how he's able to run so fast. He'll mumble something about training and discipline and plenty of early nights.

Yes, but how? Come on. How *exactly* do you run so fast?

Don't know. Something to do with the brain sending messages to the muscles?

You wouldn't, would you? Likewise, you wouldn't insist on seeing him run every time you met him and timing him to make sure he was as fast as he says he is. And if he wasn't *quite* as fast as last time you wouldn't call him a cheat and a fraud.

Of course not. Well, welcome to my world.

But you know what? Being tested is fair enough. I'm not stupid. I know that what I do defies explanation, that it's imprecise and I'm not always right, and that my profession has an end-of-the-pier image that doesn't always go hand in hand with integrity and honesty.

Which is why, when I'm tested, I stitch on the polite smile and say to Mr TV producer, 'Of course, darling, what would you like me to do?' Inside, though – that steely bit of me so few people see – I'm thinking, 'Bring it on.'

One of those who came to test me was a writer and broadcaster, Danny Penman, who was doing a piece for the *Daily Mail*. You can read his report online, but basically, he came along for a reading himself before sending along some anonymous test subjects. For his reading I was able to tell him a lot of stuff I could not have known – about his holiday to Greece, a job his girlfriend had accepted and even a dispute involving his parents. As you've probably gathered, I call them 'hits'. Apologies if that doesn't sound very mystical but there you go – his interview was full of them and he left thoroughly perplexed about what I was able to do.

Then there were the three 'test subjects' prepared by him. I gave readings for all of them, one by phone, and on all of them I had a significant number of hits. I told one woman that she had a connection with a brutal murder she didn't even know about until later. She was blown away. The other two were forced to admit that they were impressed despite themselves. No, I didn't get everything right – believe me, I never do. But every one of them came away from my reading thinking, 'How did she know that?'

Sceptics, of course, will tell you that it's cold reading. This is when you make statements that sound specific but are in fact quite general, like, 'You've just been on a journey.' All very well, but that completely ignores those times when I'm very, very specific indeed, and there are plenty of them. If, for example, I'd told Danny Penman he was 'going on a journey', that might have been cold reading, but I didn't, I told him he was going to Greece. If I'd mentioned to one of his test subjects that she had a recurring health problem then that would have been cold reading, but I didn't, I told her she had a recurring problem with her throat and guess what? Every year she loses her voice.

One of the readings was on the telephone, so that rules out the argument that we use body language. This was the woman I told about the murder, which was near a railway line. As she says in the piece, at the time she thought I was mad, but later it turned out that she did in fact have a connection with a girl stabbed by a railway line. I told her that she lived in a house that I thought was once a dairy – I could see it piled high with crates and bottles. In fact, she lives in a converted brewery. I told her that a spirit called Hilly, Tilly or Millie lived there and that she was fascinated by electricity. There was a lady called Millie who died in her house, and the electricity often flickers on and off.

Just a whole bunch of lucky guesses, I suppose. The other possibility, of course, is that I obtained the information beforehand. I didn't, of course, but let's for a moment assume that's my method. Then how? How on earth could I get this kind of detailed information? I'd need a network of highly trained, discreet private detectives and I wonder what one of those charges by the hour – certainly more than I charge for a reading. I've heard it said that we have 'teams' of investigators. Not just one. *Teams* of them. Do me a favour.

Believe me, it's not guessing, it's not intuition or insight, it's not cheating. It is what it is. When I was in Australia I did a reading for a woman and the name Tup came up. I asked the woman if she ran Tupperware parties. She shook her head. No, she didn't run Tupperware parties and I could see from her face that she was thinking, 'What on earth is she going on about?' So I said, 'Well, why do I keep hearing the word Tup, then?'

It turned out to be her dead husband's name.

Now how did I get that? A woman I don't know in the middle of Australia. I don't think I even had the internet then, so researching is out. I've never even heard Tup as a name before so that rules out cold reading, too, doesn't it?

That's the thing with sceptics. They pride themselves on questioning everything, but what they don't stop to question is how we psychics are supposed to be pulling off this huge fraud. I said earlier that psychics are sometimes guilty of throwing out too-easy answers to tough questions. Well, so are sceptics if you ask me. They'll tell you that cold reading and research covers everything we do, but it doesn't. Some things can't be explained.

Which is what Danny Penman concluded. He didn't come away from his experiment believing in the paranormal. Instead, he had what I find is a common reaction: that what I do defies explanation.

It does. It certainly does.

And if there's one thing I've learnt myself, it's that. I said earlier that I hoped by writing this book, my life might start to make some kind sense to me. As I near the end, does it? I'm not sure.

Some things just cannot be explained.

And yet again, with the publication of Danny Penman's article, I found myself in the papers. People were scratching their heads over what I could do. Once more I found myself mingling with celebrities as I was invited to appear at a birthday party arranged for George Michael by his partner, Kenny Goss. Goodness, what a night that was. Arriving at the house, just as beautiful as you'd expect, I was greeted by Kenny in his (you guessed it) bathrobe, before being shown outside to where the party was being staged. Imagine. There were little wooden bridges, streams, the trees were festooned with lights and there were floral decorations everywhere. The food being laid out was like nothing I'd ever seen before. I was to hold court, giving readings in my own tent, and sure enough when the party got going I soon had a marquee full of A-list types wanting a reading. Of course, it would be indiscreet of me to say exactly who, as many of them then became clients.

Afterwards, a florist friend approached to tell me

I should see the swimming pool, which she had filled with flowers and tea lights. What a job she'd done. It was magnificent – like something out of the Chelsea Flower Show. As we approached I took John's hand and there was something about that moment. It was dusk, candle-light was glinting from the surface of the water and behind us from the lawn was the sound of music, conversation and laughter. What it was, I realized, I felt happy. Truly happy. As though this moment was somehow payment for everything I'd had to endure in order to reach it.

We wandered down to the side of the pool where there were loungers and sat on one, just enjoying the pool, listening to the sounds of the party. Over the way was a pool house, inside it a little mini-party, things still relatively quiet, though it had the air of a party that was just warming up. We looked at each other and grinned.

I wonder, I thought, looking out at the pool (I don't think I'll ever get over how beautiful it looked), I wonder if this is what the spirit world meant for me. If it's placed me here, either to say thank you for the hardships of the past, or – oh bloody hell, here's a thought – to butter me up for hardship to come.

Either way, I thought, thank you. It hasn't been an easy journey, but there aren't many who have had the life I have. It certainly hasn't been short on eventful moments, that much is for certain.

'Hello, Sally.'

Oh my gawd, it was George Michael.

Well, if you have to be torn out of a reverie by anyone, it might as well be him, eh?

He sat down beside John and me and we chewed the fat for a moment or so. There were so many guests at this party, it was nice just to have a few minutes of his time. At his request I read for him, and for a moment or so he fought back tears. They were happy tears, I think. I didn't have any bad news for him, let's put it that way. And then off he went, with one parting shot.

'You will stay, Sally,' he insisted.

But I had clients the next day and it was gone midnight.

'No, sorry, love, I've got to get going.'

'Are you sure?' he said. 'The party's only just getting started.'

It is, I thought, as we pulled away from his party and back to home, to reality. The party's only just getting started.

Epilogue

Not long ago, I wrote to Jemma. It was a new beginning that came to nothing for a variety of reasons too painful to go into. I am still estranged from her, and that hurting in my heart will never leave me – not while she remains out of my life.

I did it because something happened to me that made me realize I had to; a journey that started, funnily enough, when I was making the beds one day and I had a thought, a vision, a knowing.

It said, Derek West is your father.

Westy.

I don't know. Was it a psychic knowing, or was it the penny dropping after all those years of hints and stories and evasions from mum? The biggest one that had persisted was that Derek West was Gina's dad, Pat was mine. That was what I had grown up believing and what I still believed until . . . well, just a short time ago.

That day among the bed linen I suddenly knew the truth – or thought I did.

But if he was my dad, did I really want that? After all, some of those stories. There was an incident she used to tell me about when she and Westy were arguing and my mum was getting the better of him, which is no surprise because if anybody had the gift of the gab it was her. I was a babe in arms, only just able to sit up, and he grabbed me, took me out into the street, sat me in the middle of the road and went back inside.

'Where's Sally?' she demanded of him. She'd heard the door open and close and assumed he'd put me out the front in my pram, which was what you did back in those days (and here I am, right at the end and still talking about the old days – just not the good old days). But when she went to the front door and poked her head out there was no pram, just this crying sound from the middle of the road where I sat.

'*Sally.*'

Did I really want a man like that as my dad?

All the same, I rang him.

'It's Sally here,' I said, 'do you remember Sally and Gina?'

'Oh my God,' he was almost screaming down the phone. 'Is your mother dead?'

He really loved her. I felt the emotion of it down the line. Oh my God, he really loved her. So many people fell under her spell. My fathers (both of them), my sister . . . my daughter.

'She's not, no,' I said.

'Oh.'

There was a pause.

It wasn't exactly the most emotional reunion in the world. It wasn't a reunion at all, really.

'I always expected your call if . . . you know . . . if anything happened to your mother.'

'I just felt I should call you.'

'Right.'

'What happened?' I asked him. I wanted to know everything and before I knew it he was telling me about the toys he used to send for Gina and me, '. . . but your mother put them in the bin.'

'You hit her. You were abusive to her.'

'It was a long time ago, Sal.'

'That don't make it right.'

'But I know you're mine. You and Gina. I know it.'

He was right, as it turned out.

We formed a relationship, of sorts. But not long later, he died. At the funeral I met my half-brothers and sisters, the Wests, and got on well with them – something that became a bit of a sticking point with my mum.

My half-brothers and sisters used to tell me I shared characteristics with Derek. I began to feel as though I had to know. I'd embarked on a new relationship with a new set of people.

I didn't want this relationship to be built on a foundation of lies.

So one night, I got on to Google, found somewhere that does DNA tests and rang them the following morning.

'I've got a sister and we have the same mum, but we've been brought up believing that we haven't got the same dad.'

'Right,' said the DNA technician.

'I can't ask my mum and dad for DNA,' I told him.

I wasn't talking to them, of course. I'd been the Princess of Wales' psychic, been to Paris with the De Niros, watched Reggie Kray bury a man alive and read for George Michael by the side of his pool. None of these experiences I was able to share with my mum.

'And I don't want my half-brothers and sisters – if that's what they turn out to be – I don't want them knowing I'm doing this.'

'Okay . . .'

'What if I get it from my sister?' I asked. 'Could you tell then?'

'Absolutely,' he said, slowly and confidently down the phone. 'In a court of law, they will accept a 70 per cent match. But to be honest, if you get a 60 to 72 per cent match it's enough to convince us.'

'Not 100? You can never be 100 per cent?'

'No, not if you're not twins.'

And that was that. I did the test.

Six weeks later, the phone rang. Believe me, I'd been busy in that period. Clients, magazines, TV. My *Star Psychic* series on ITV was still a glint in my eye but even so, things were going mad. A snowball that just wouldn't stop, and wouldn't, really, until a couple of years later, when *Star Psychic* came out. Mind you, what am I talking about? It still hasn't stopped, touch wood.

'Oh, hello, bloody hell, I'd forgotten all about you. How long has it been?'

'It's been about six or seven weeks. I have your results.'

'Oh, great, when will I receive them?'

Dumb, Sally, really dumb.

'No, I have them in front of me.'

'What? You mean, you can give them to me?'

'Yes.'

'Oh,' and I paused, realizing that I wanted Pat to be my dad. I'd grown up believing he was my dad and Gina belonged to Derek. That was the way the world had worked for me. Never mind psychic knowings or the things my mum had told me growing up. With a sudden yearning feeling I wanted my childhood to remain where it was: fixed in that time and place at Waldemar Avenue, where mum was mum and dad was dad. No matter how bad it had been. In that moment, that's all I wanted. I wanted there to be no more secrets. I wanted it so that when mum had yelled at Derek West, 'They're not yours,' she'd been telling the truth.

To have found out otherwise would have been like hearing the earth was flat, the sky is green, the grass is pink. Not right, not right.

'Well when we do this test, it is very rare, even with twins, that we get the results that we've got with you,' he said.

'Right,' I said, 'so what does that mean?'

It means, he told me, that the earth is flat, the sky is green and the grass is pink: 'You have the same parentage. You definitely have the same parentage as your sister. It is 99.99 per cent certain that you have the same parentage.'

My head was swimming, I felt woozy, the room went to blancmange around me.

'What does that mean?' I heard myself say.

'Sally, it means you have the same mother and father as your sister. This, um, Derek West? He's your father.'

When I put down the phone everything had changed. It was as though I was being shown the same film of my childhood, only now I was seeing it from a completely new angle. Everything I had heard. Years and years of secrets.

Now I knew the truth.

For crying out loud, I'm a psychic, I thought. I sit down opposite a person and I know what they had for bleedin' lunch, and for all these years I didn't know that Derek West was dad and Pat was not.

On the other hand, Derek was dead and I never spoke to Pat. At the end of the day, did it really matter? It probably didn't. The real wrong done was not knowing.

But all those skeletons in the cupboard, well, they're not in the cupboard anymore. And in the cold light of day they don't even seem like skeletons anymore. Not in the sense that they're frightening, or sinister; they're just bits of old bones, cluttering the place up. Because that's what happens. You face up to these things and suddenly . . . I don't know, it's as if they lose their power somewhat. Their grip weakens. The hard bit is opening that cupboard in the first place.

But I did it. And looking back over my life now – writing this book and revisiting some of those skeletons – I know that everything I've been through has helped me in my work. I'm not only a stronger person because of all that has happened but I'm a better medium. My work as a psychic – which has always been about helping people at the end of the day, that's what I do – has improved as a result. It makes me think that everything happens for a reason; that I couldn't have my gift without the accompanying hardship.

Now, though, well, I wouldn't exactly say that my life is complete – without Jemma how can it be? But at least I've reached a place where I can look back on my life and things make a kind of sense. I have beautiful children and a husband who loves me. I have a gift I can use to help people and just writing those last couple of sentences makes me realize how lucky I am. All that bad stuff – hopefully behind me at last. Time to look forward, to do what I enjoy, what I'm good at.

And yes, thanks, I've heard all the jokes about being a happy medium.